TOKYO PORN

MAGNUS BECKMAN

Tokyo Porn

Copyright © Magnus Beckman 2020

The content of this book has been curated from found photos. All photographers have been credited next to the photo used. All photography belongs to photographers.

The author and publisher shall have neither liability nor responsibility to any person or entity with respect to any loss or damage caused or alleged to be caused, directly or indirectly, by the information contained in this book or any related materials.

ISBN: 9798581417171
Imprint: Independently published

First edition November 2020

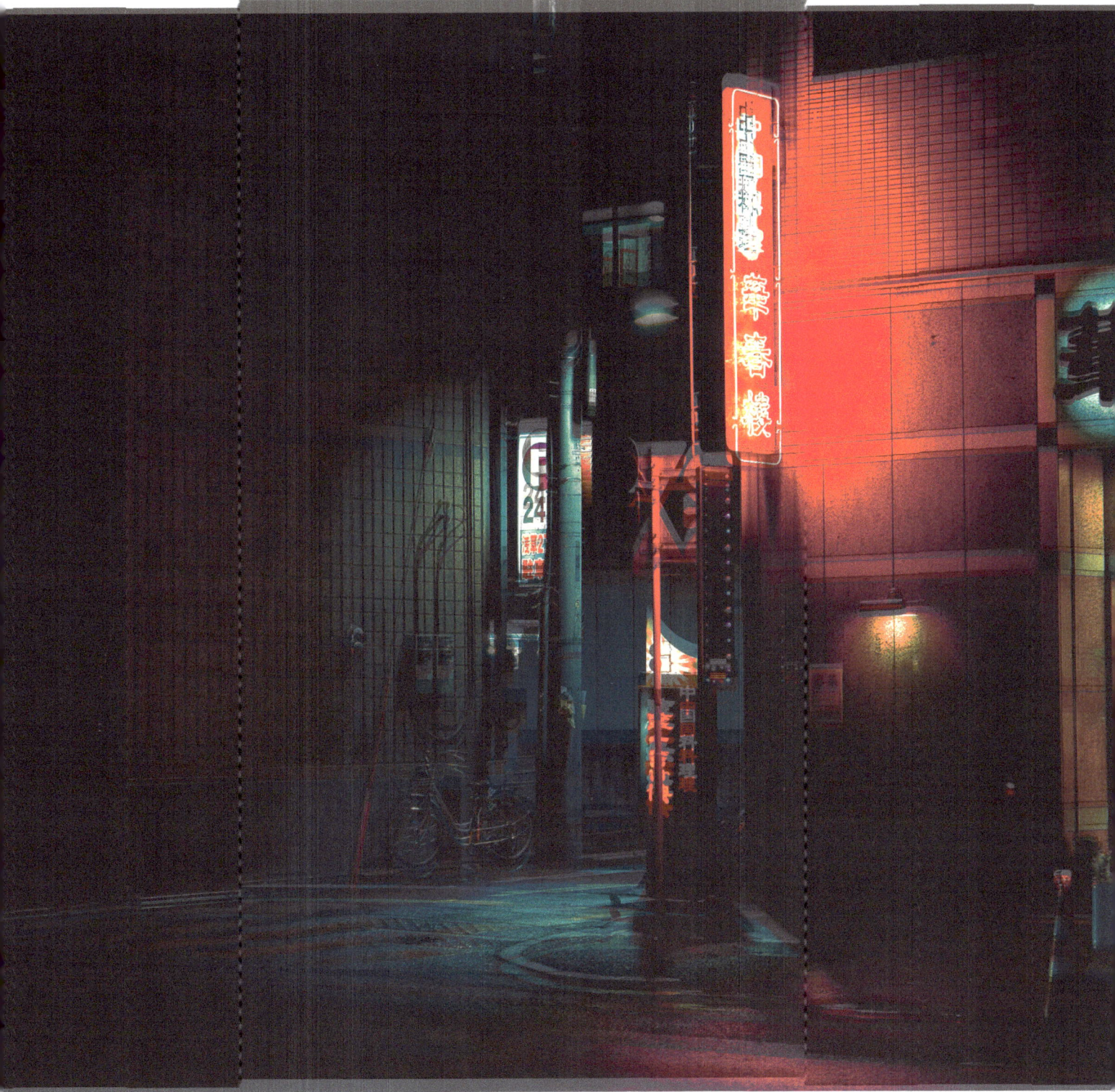

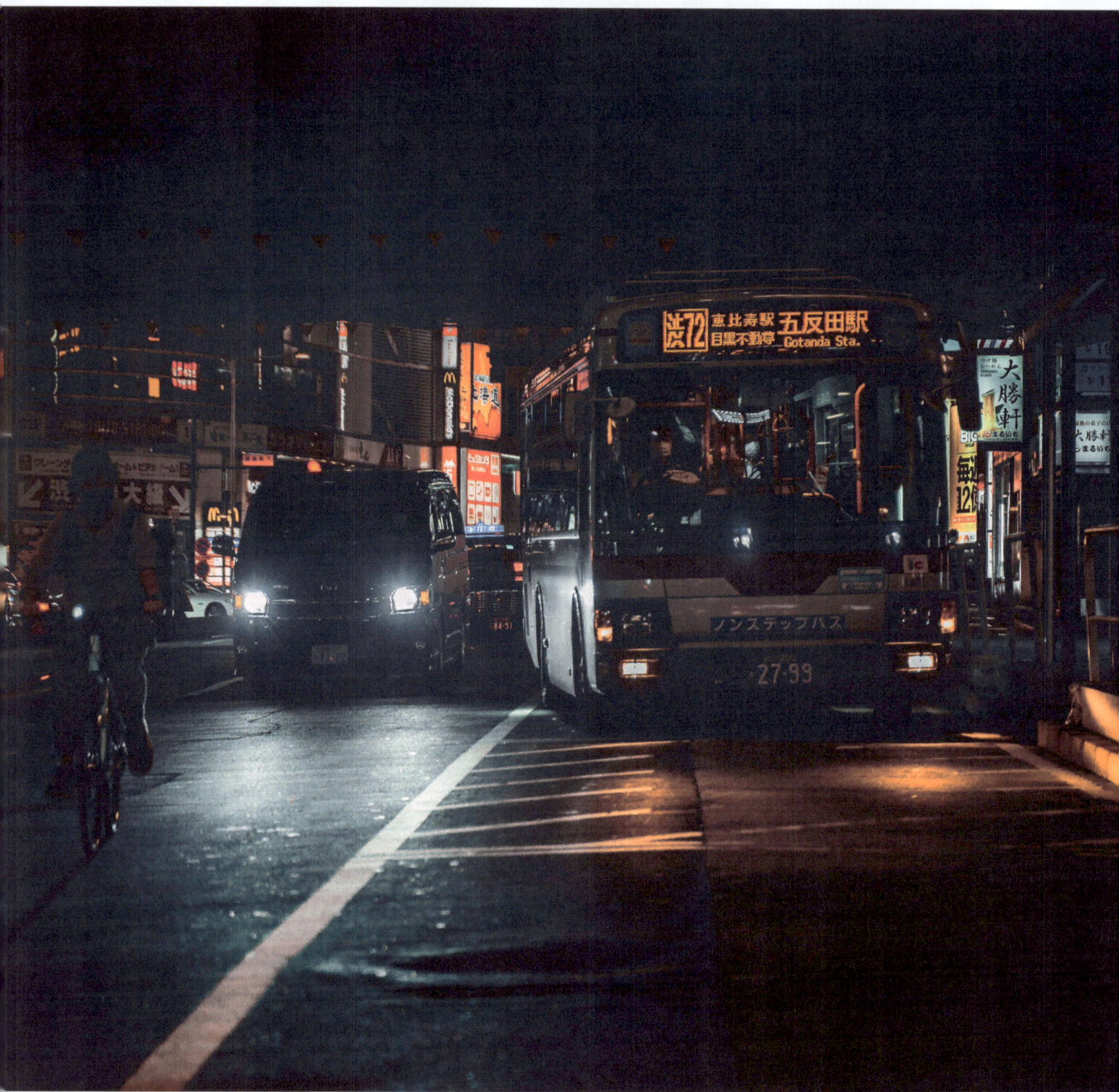
Photo by Heshan Perera

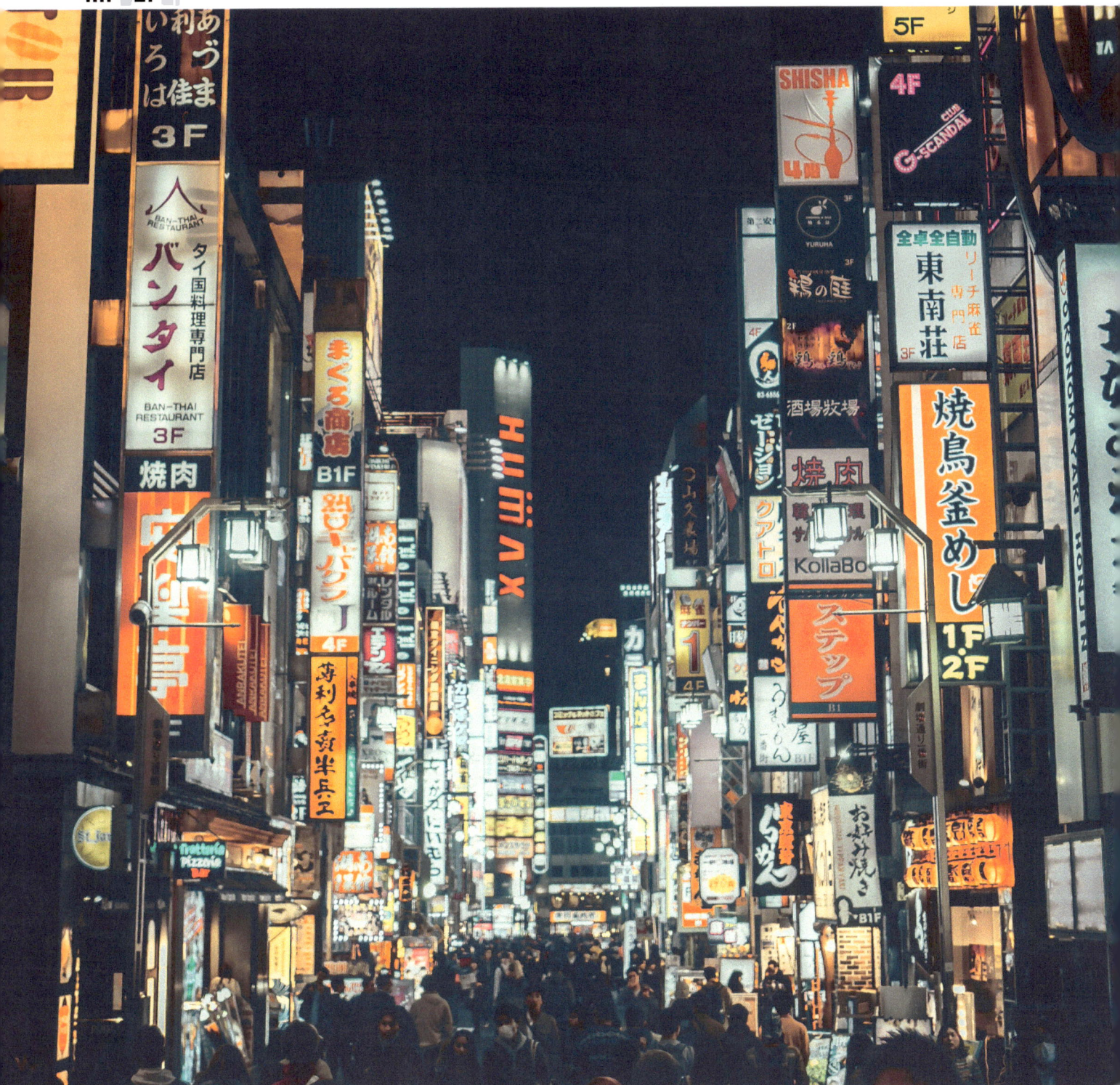
Photo by Yoav Aziz

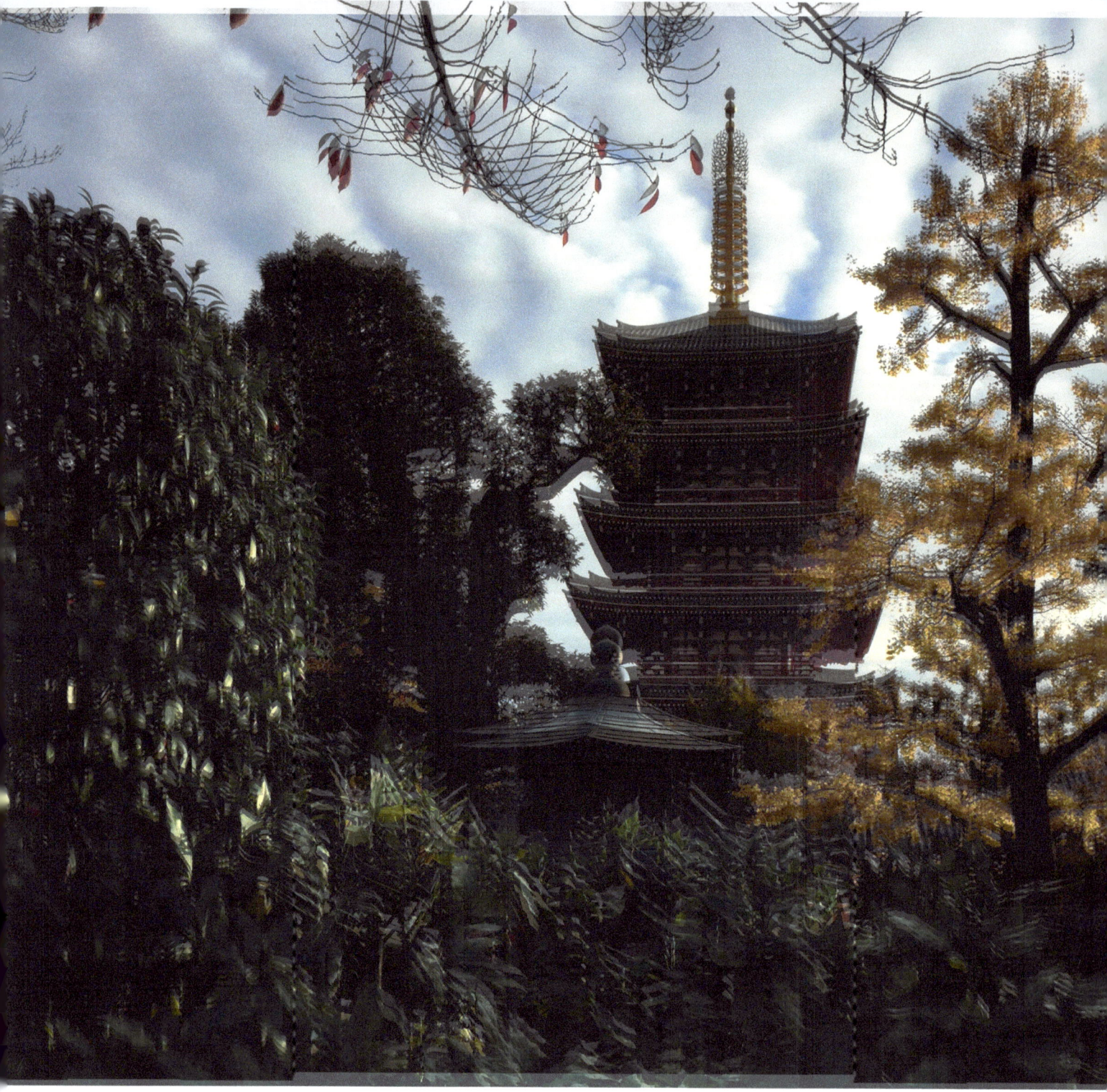
Photo by Ash Hayes

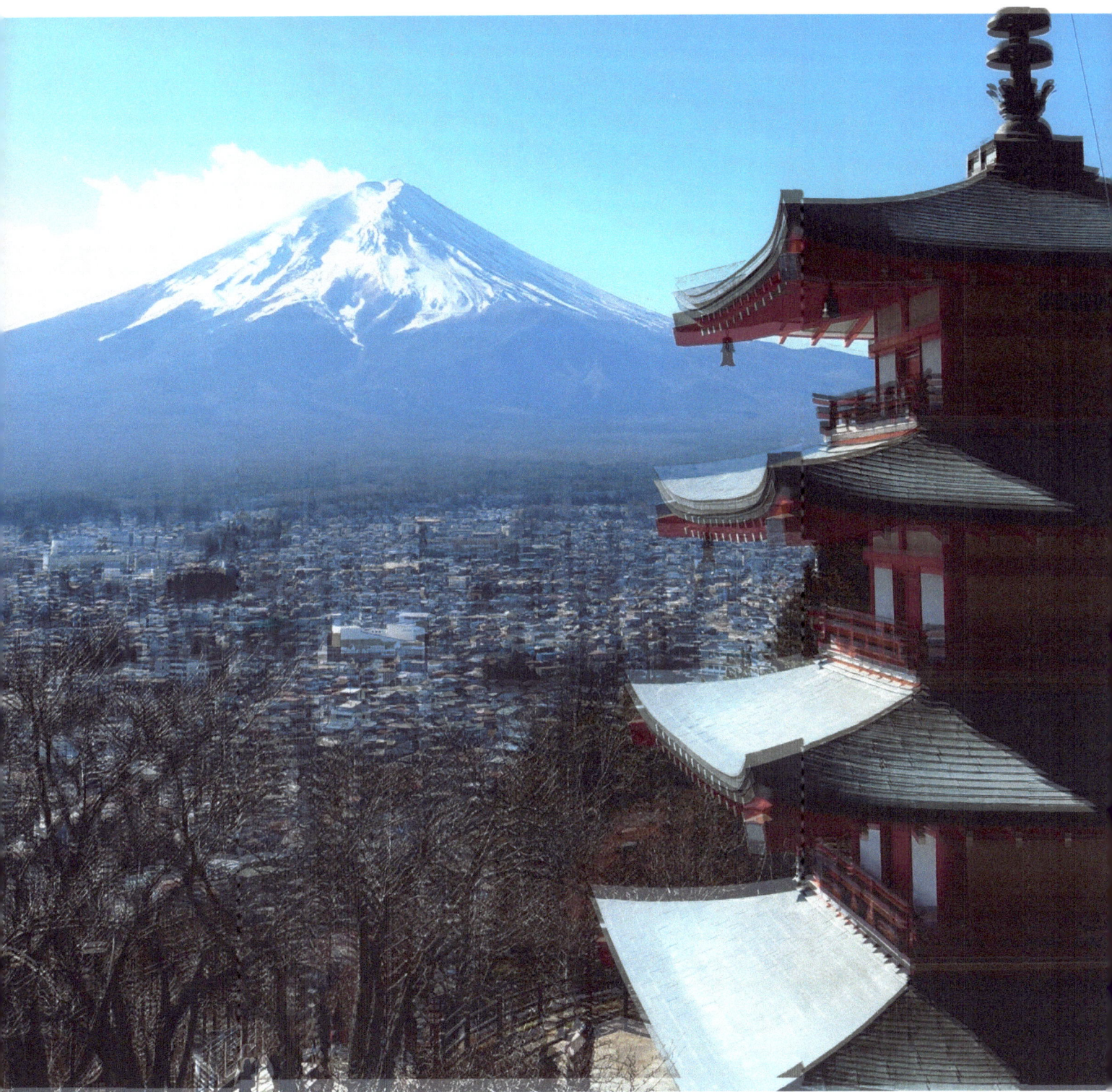
Photo by Ifan Nuriyana

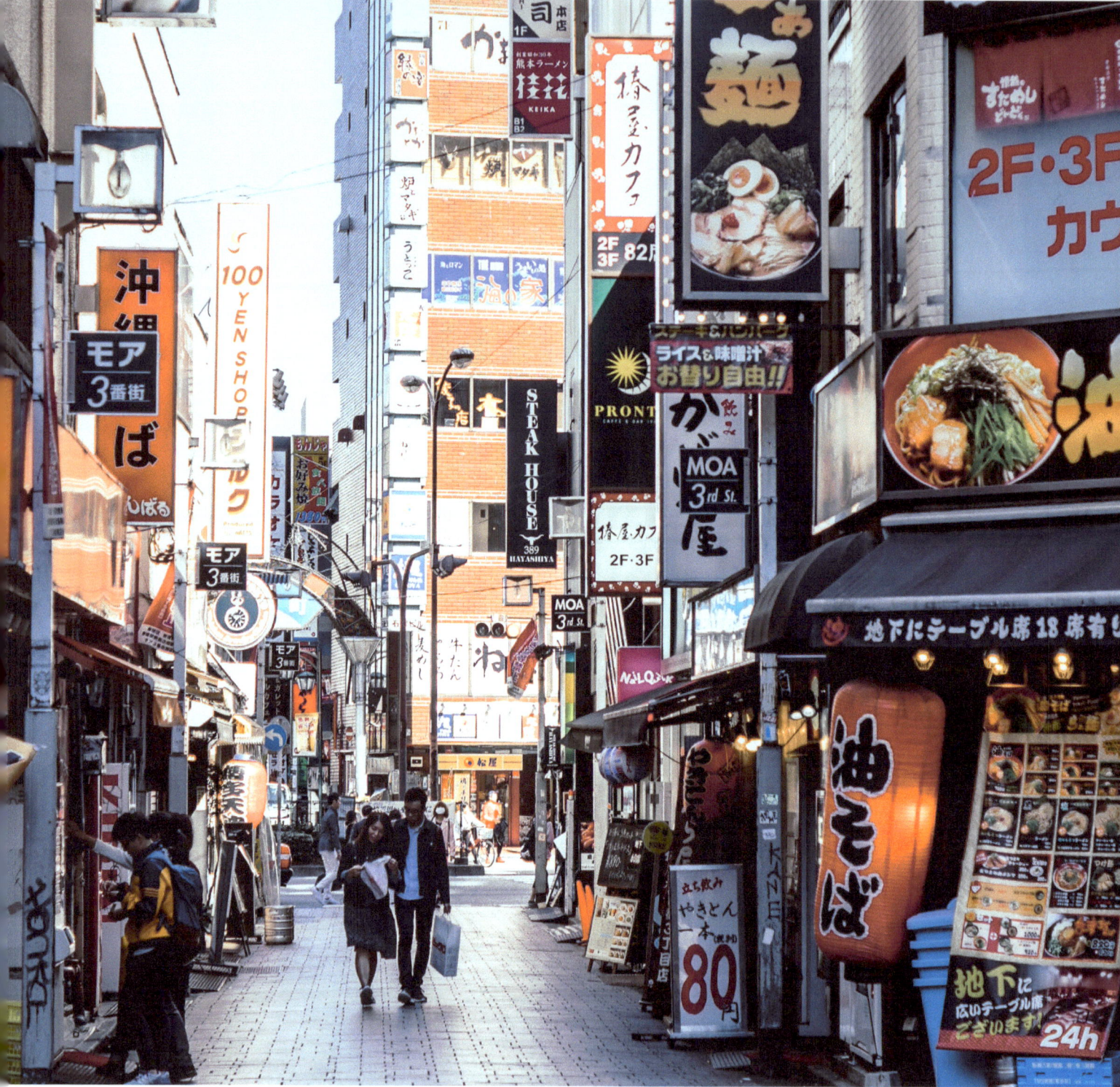
Photo by Bantersnaps

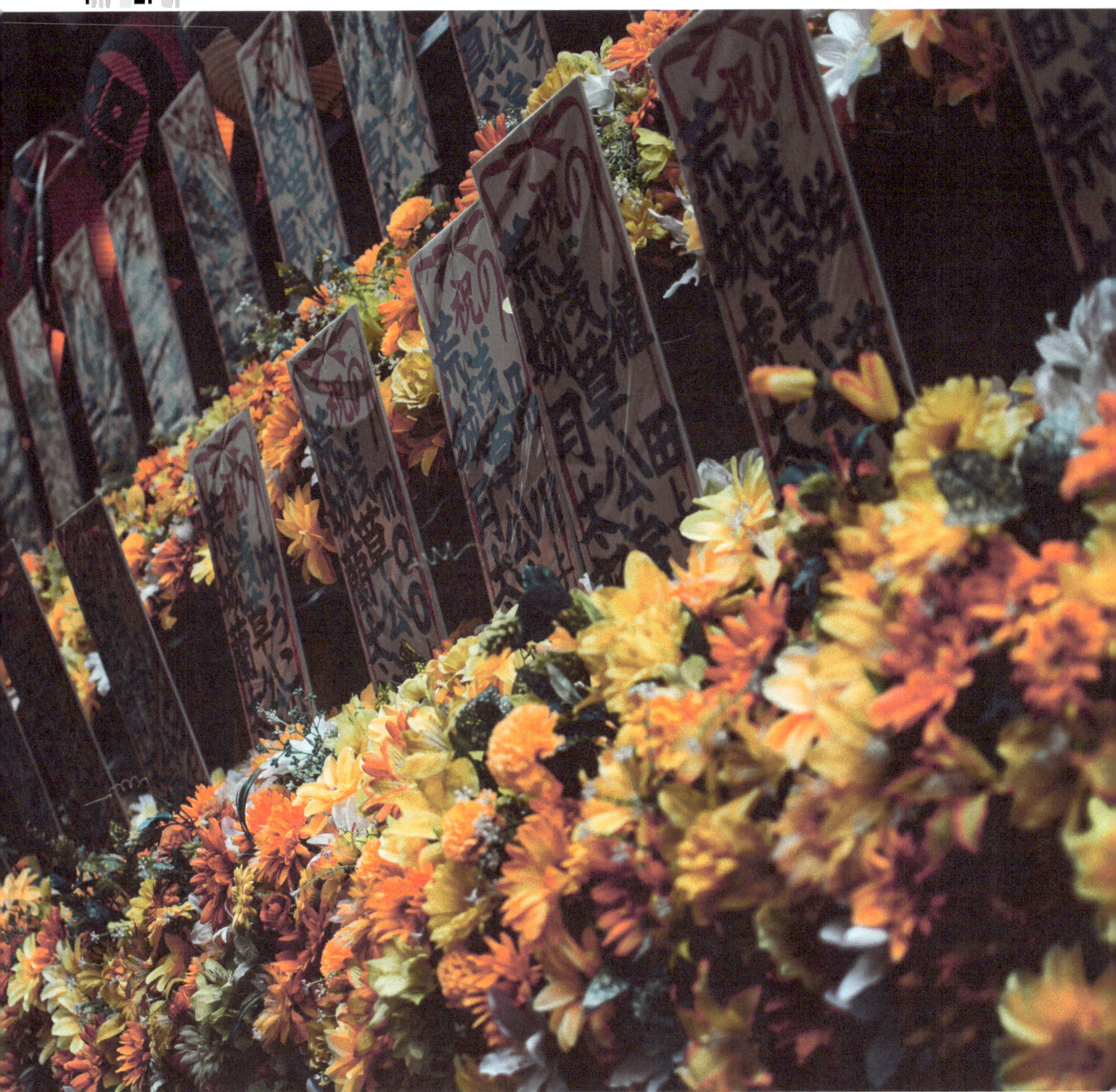

Photo by Sebastian Hages

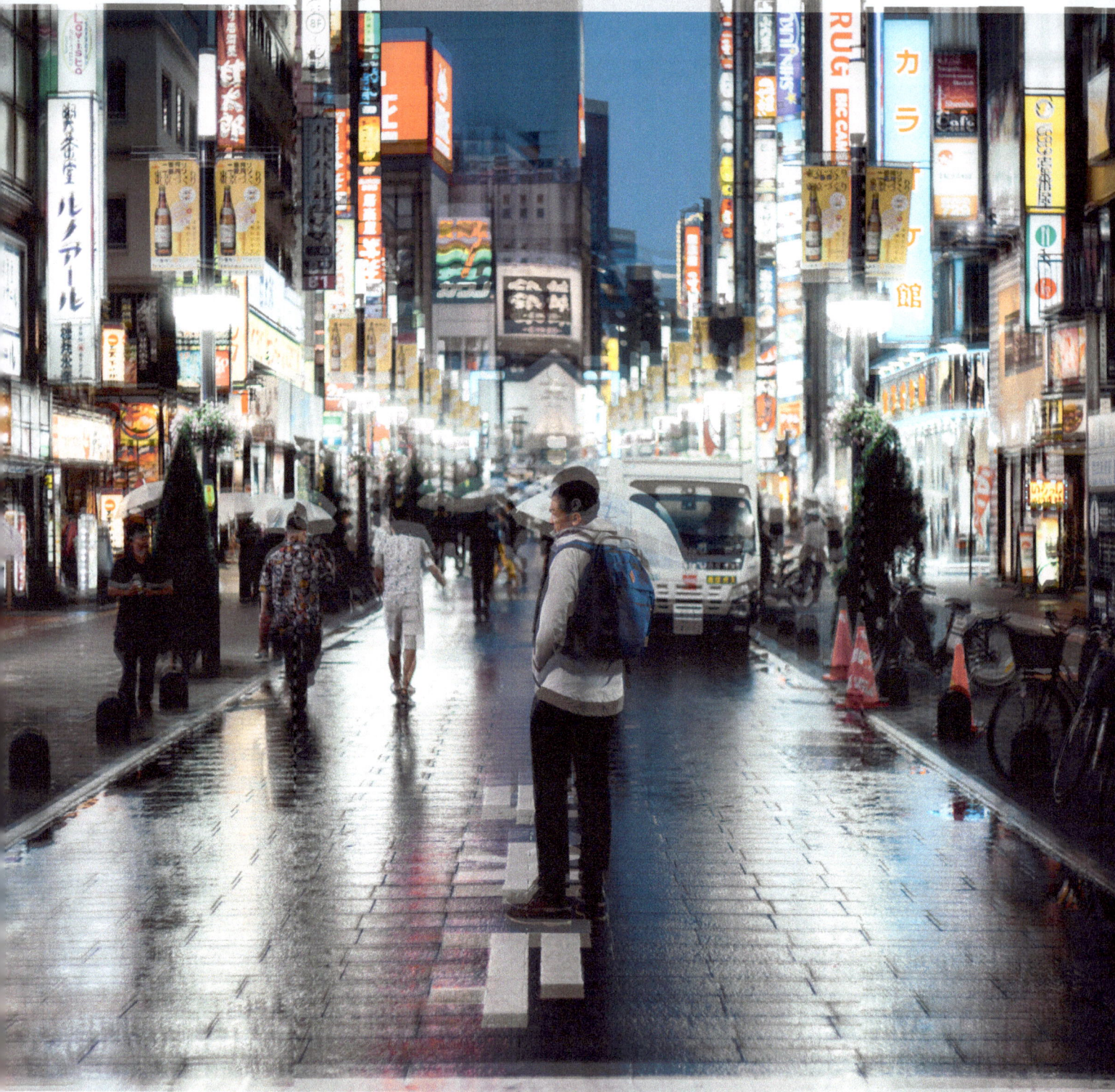
Photo by Ben Parker

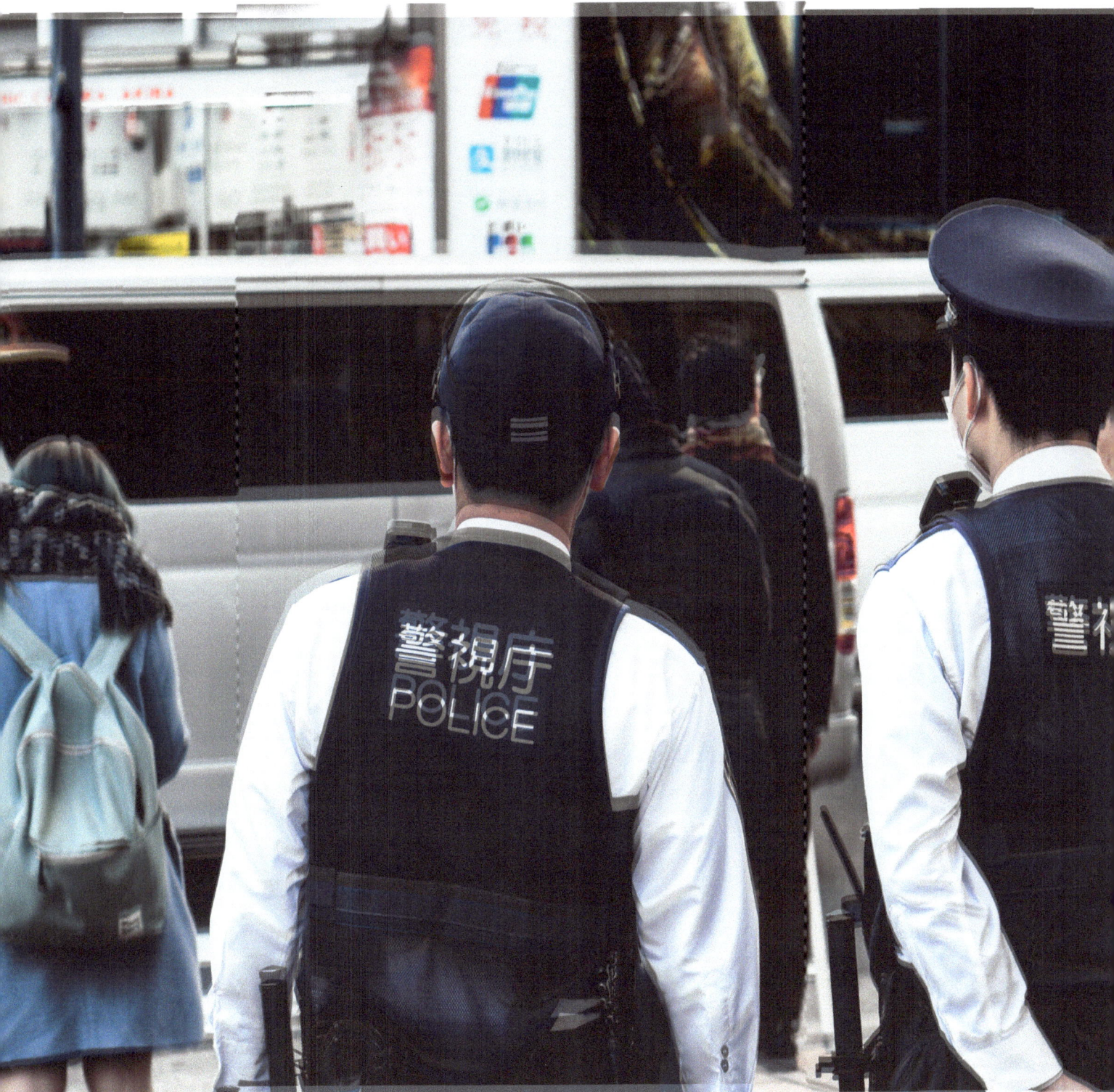
Photo by Adrien Bruneau

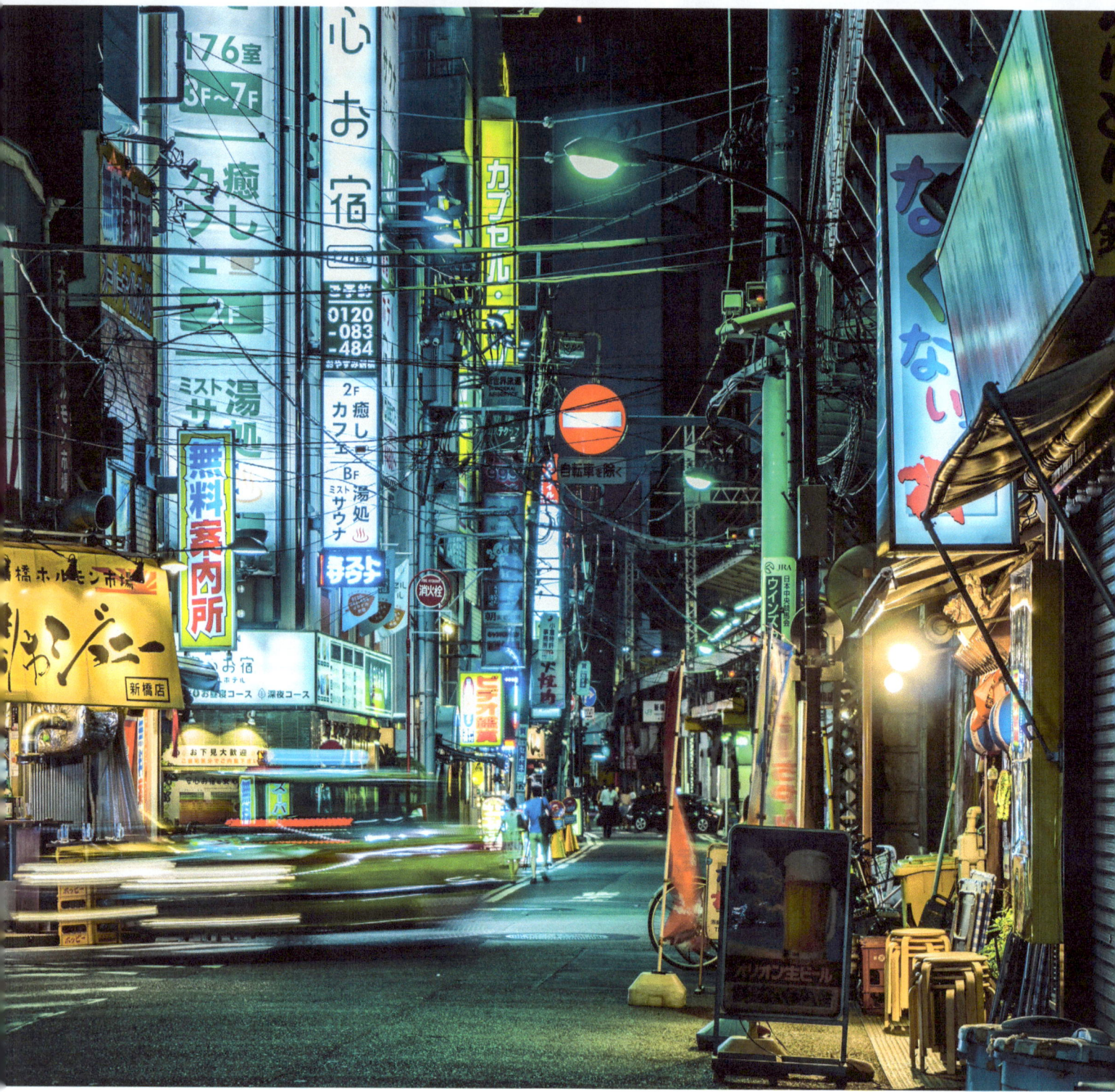

Photo by Cem Ersozlu

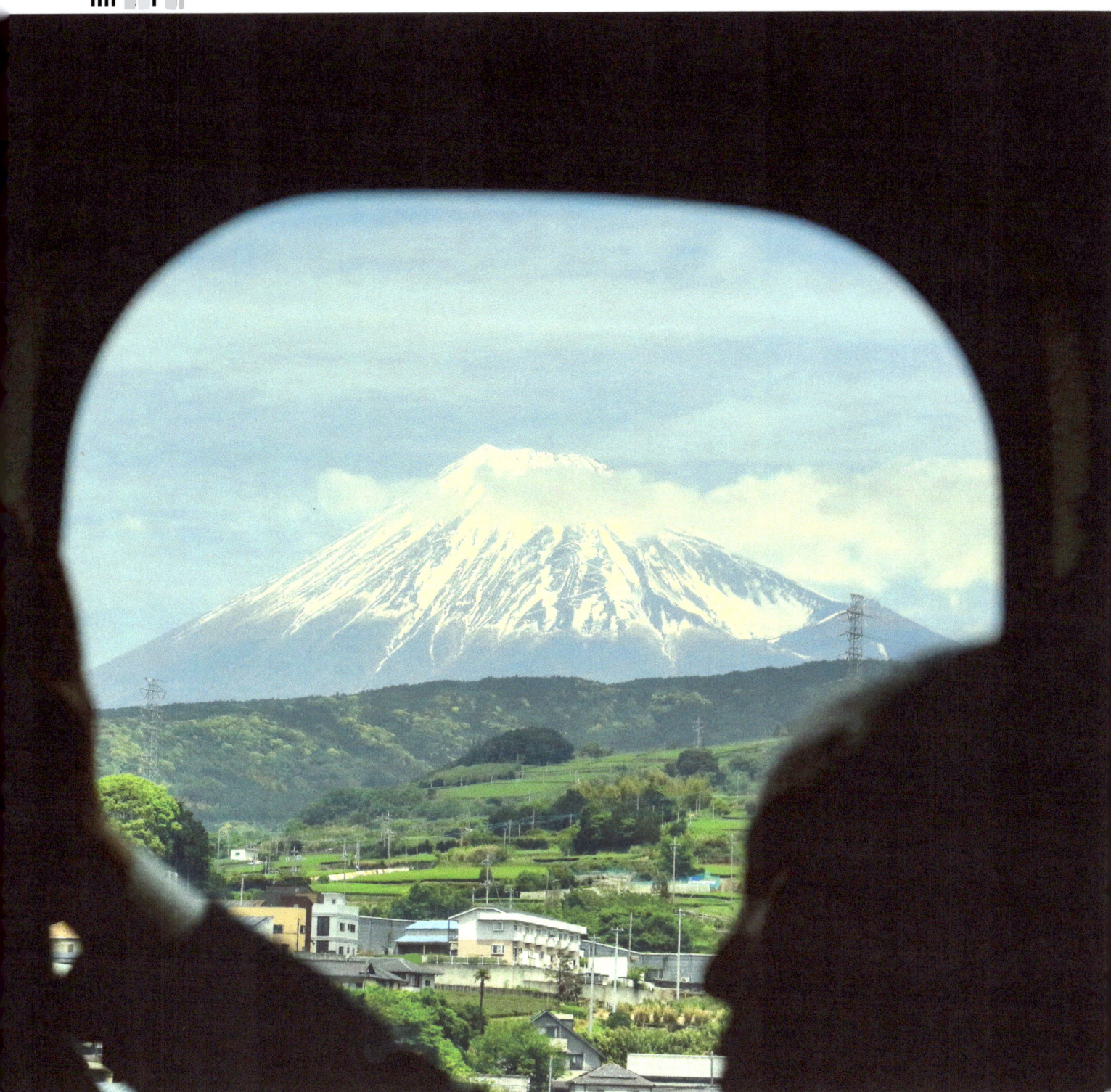

Photo by Colton Jones

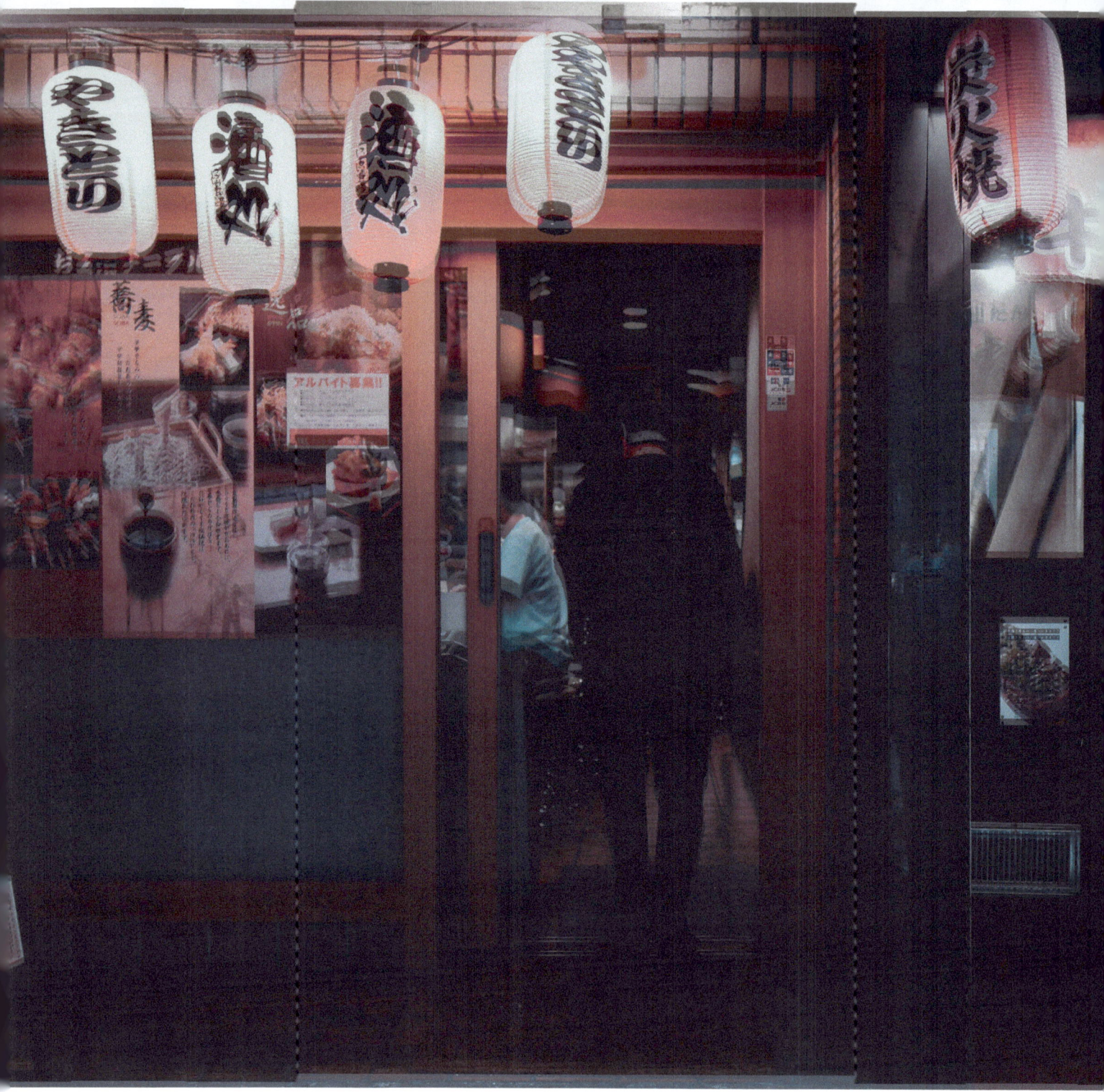

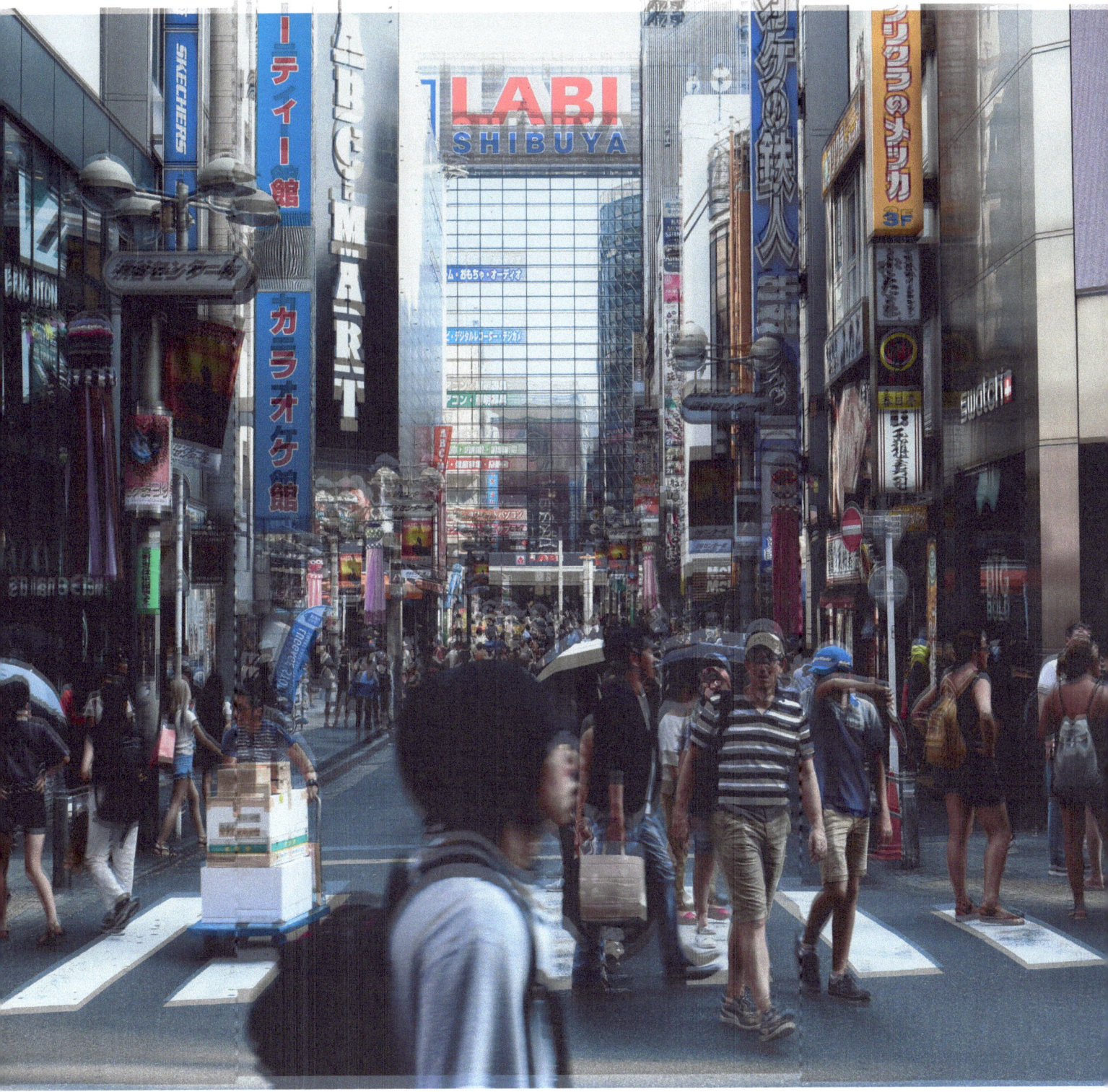
Photo by Anthony Da Cruz

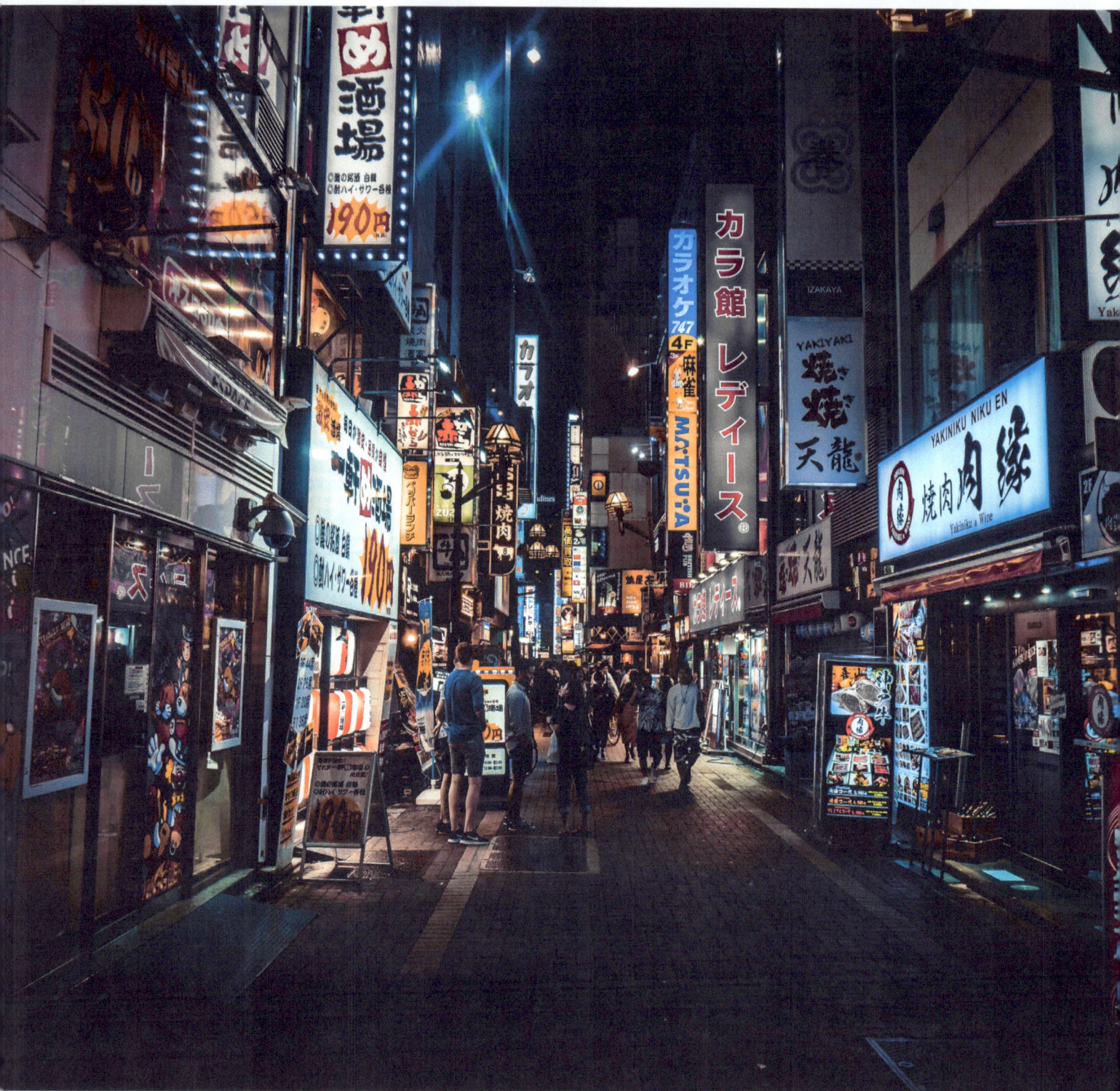
Photo by David Billings

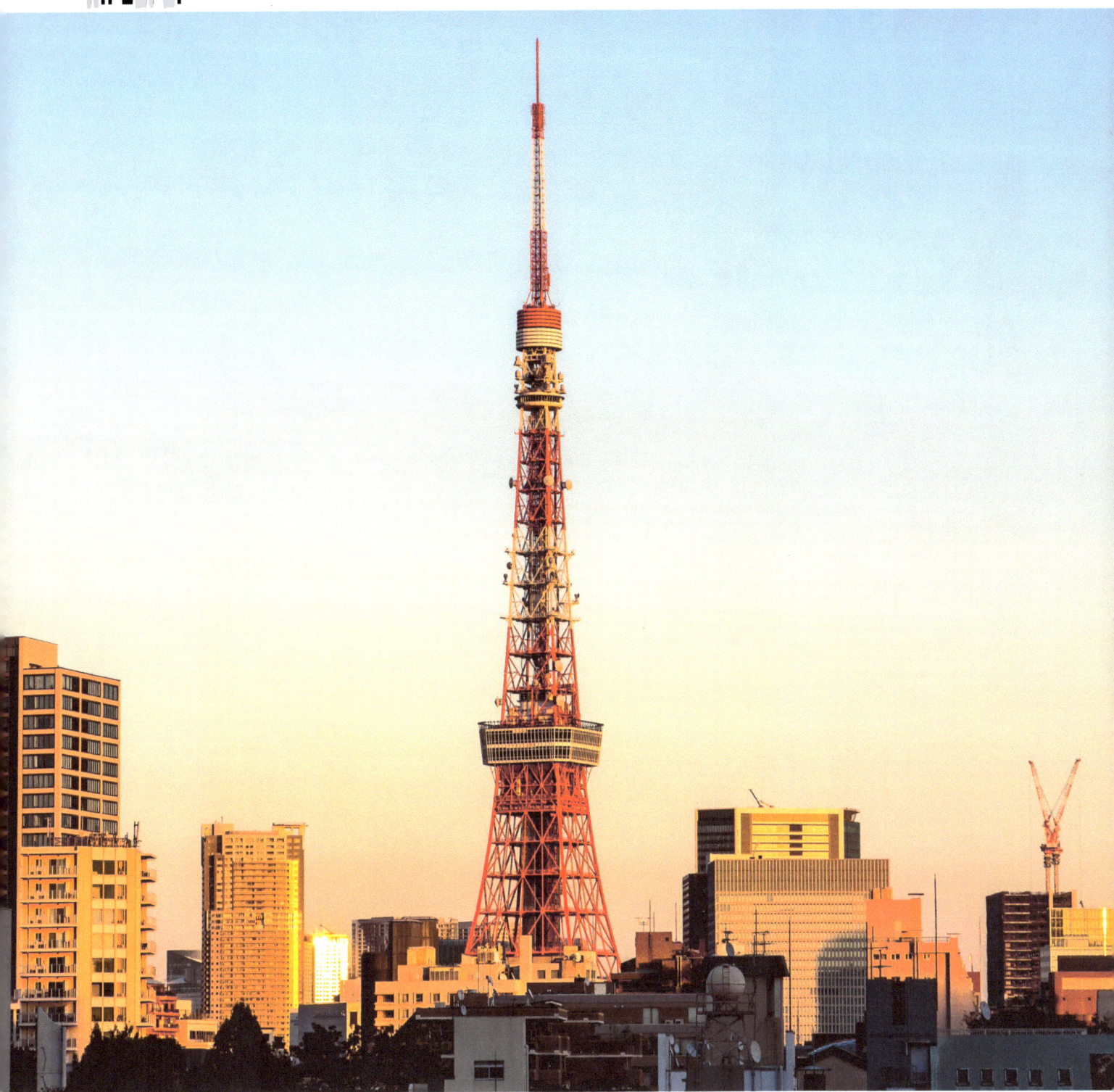
Photo by Bing Hui Yau

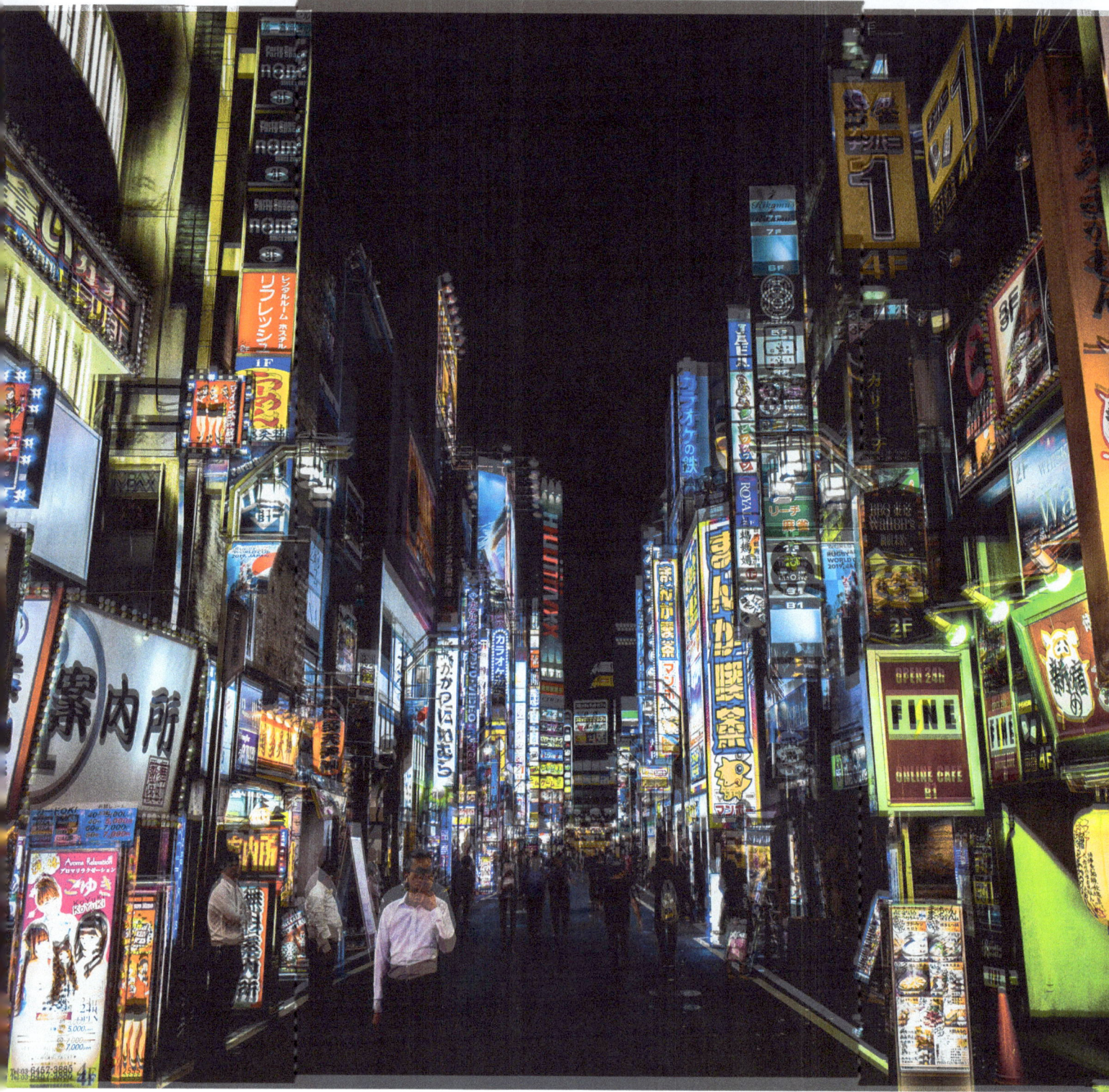

Photo by Nicholas Doherty

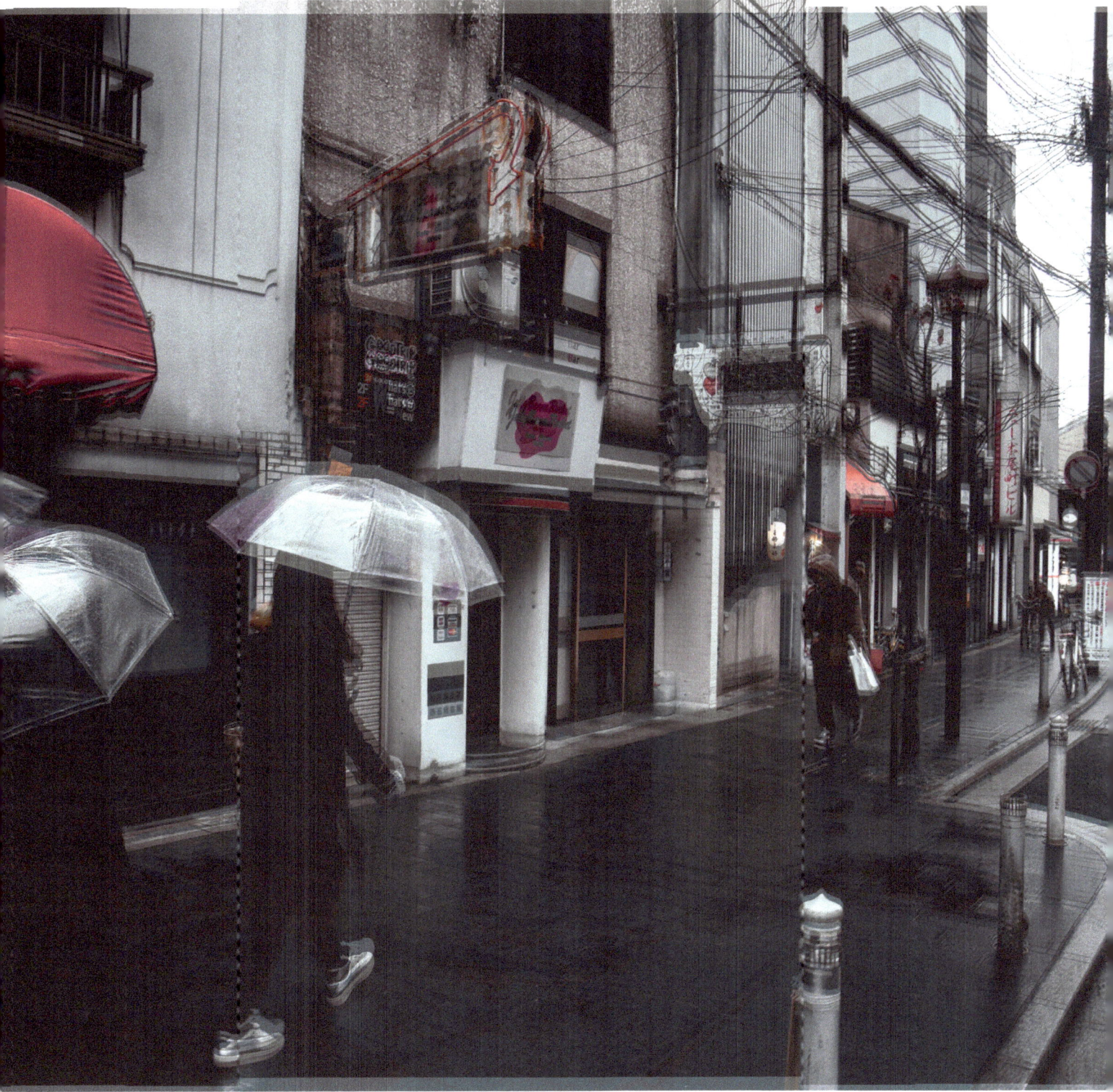

Photo by Zachariah Hagy

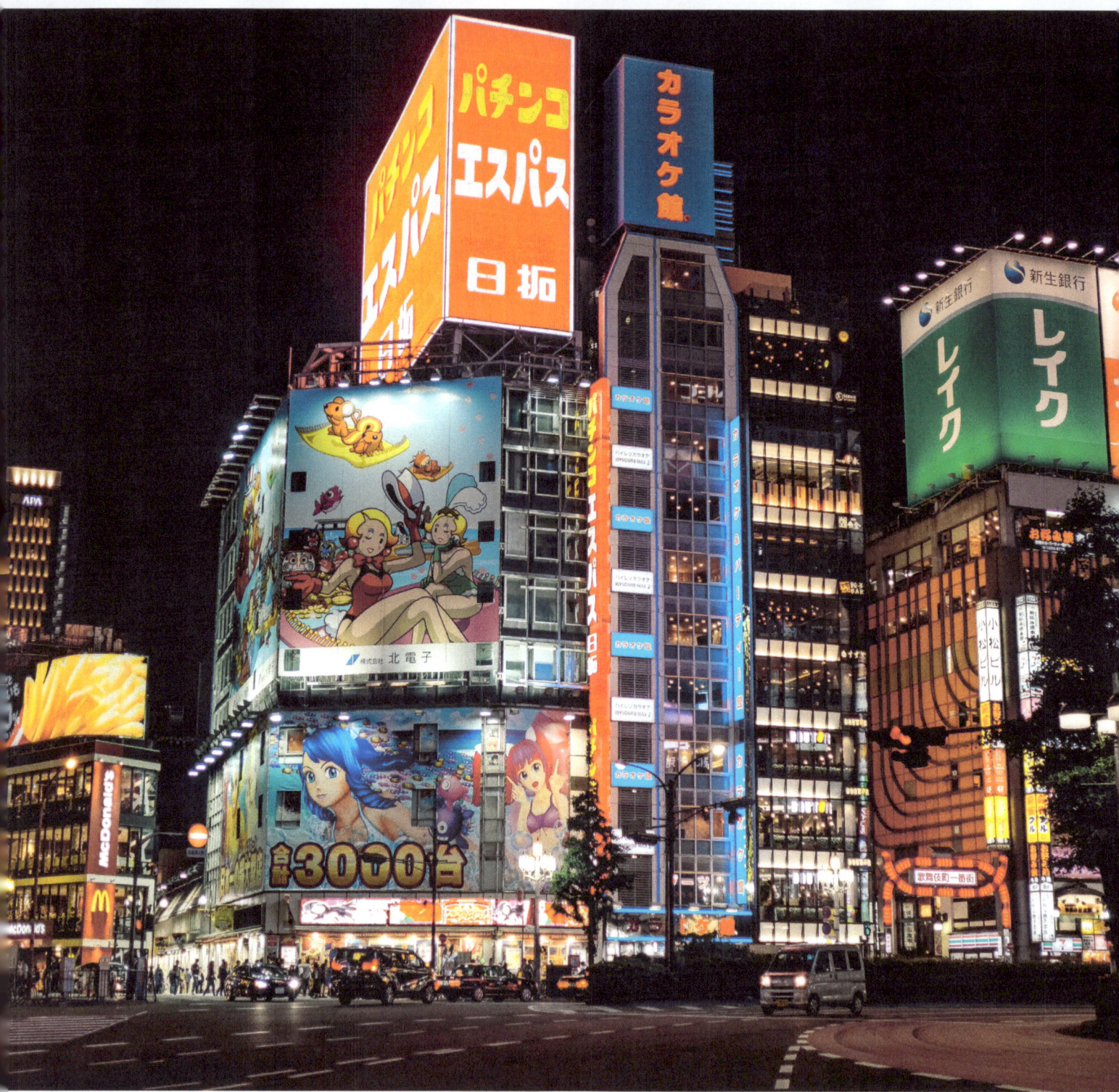

Photo by Ajay Murthy

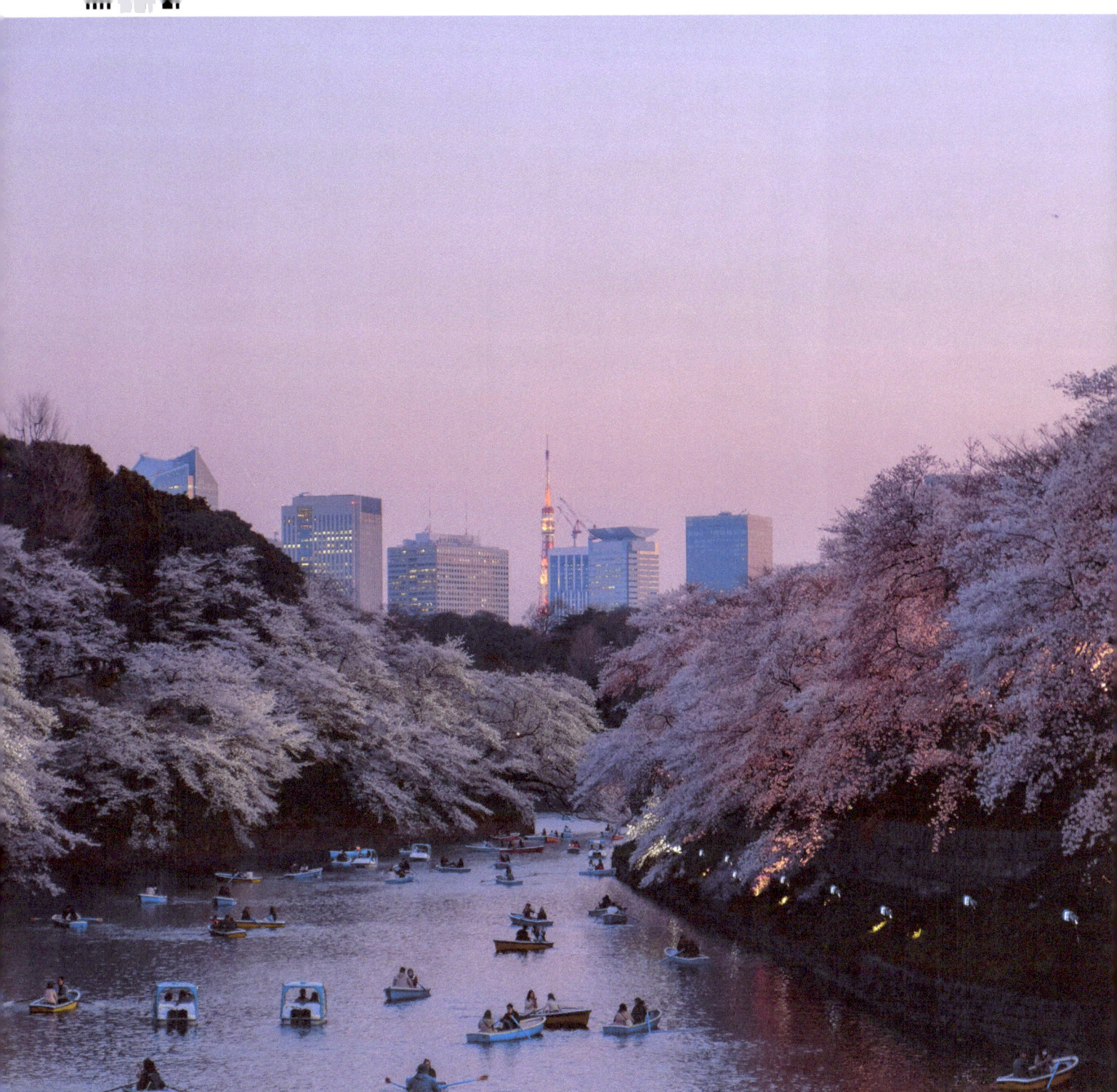
Photo by Yu Kato

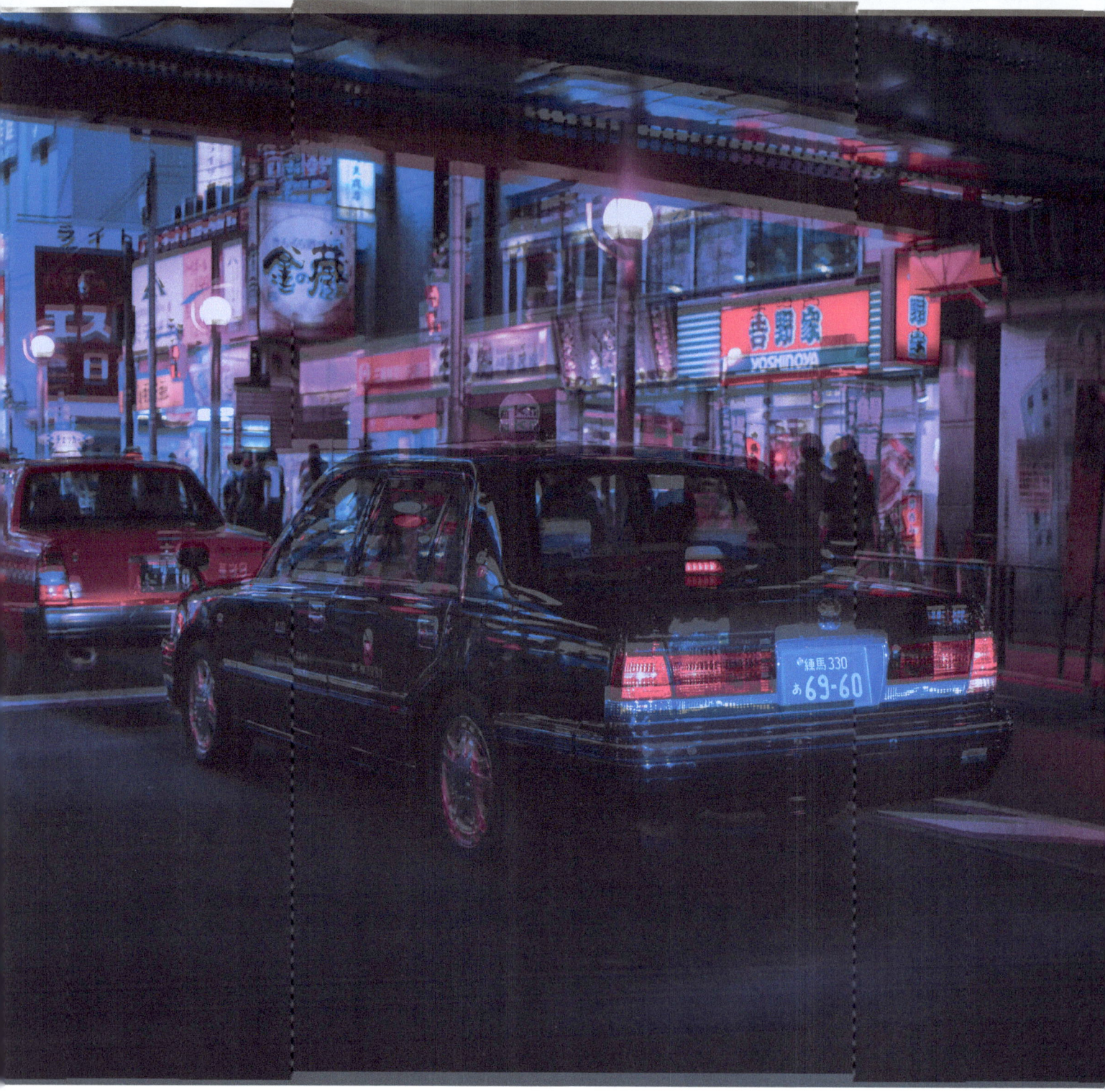

Photo by Matthieu Buhler

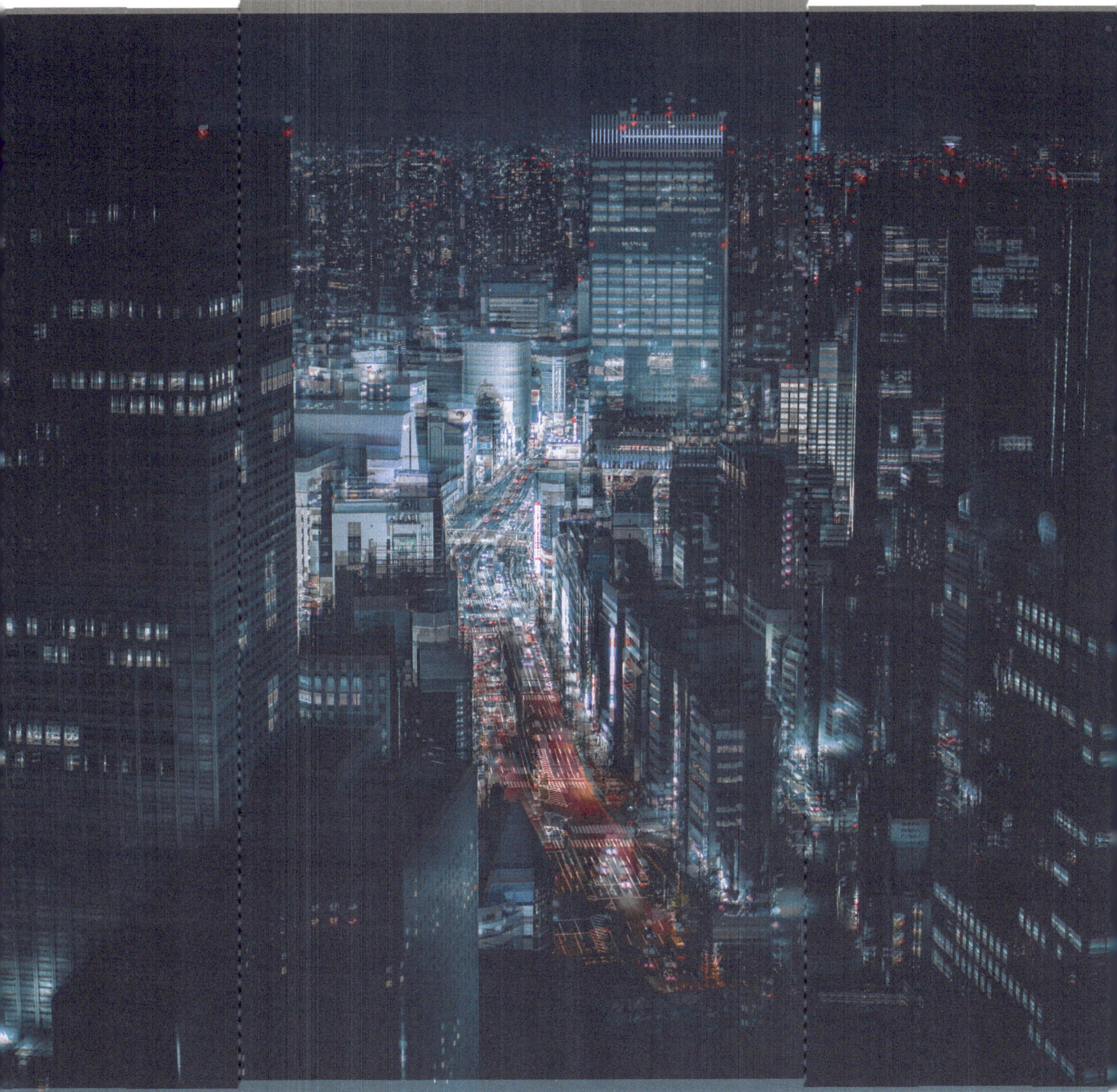

Photo by André Benz

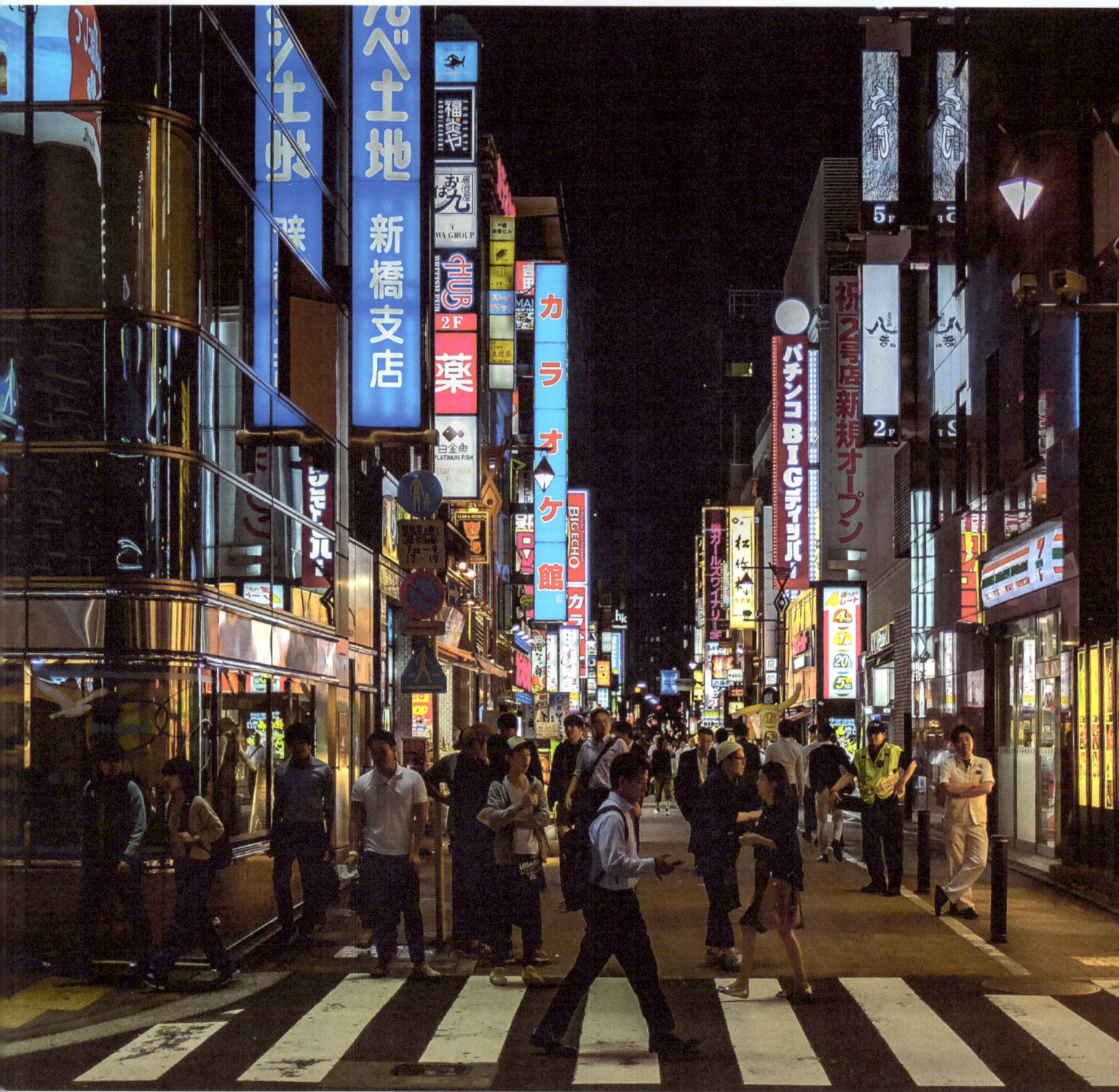
Photo by Martijn Baudoin

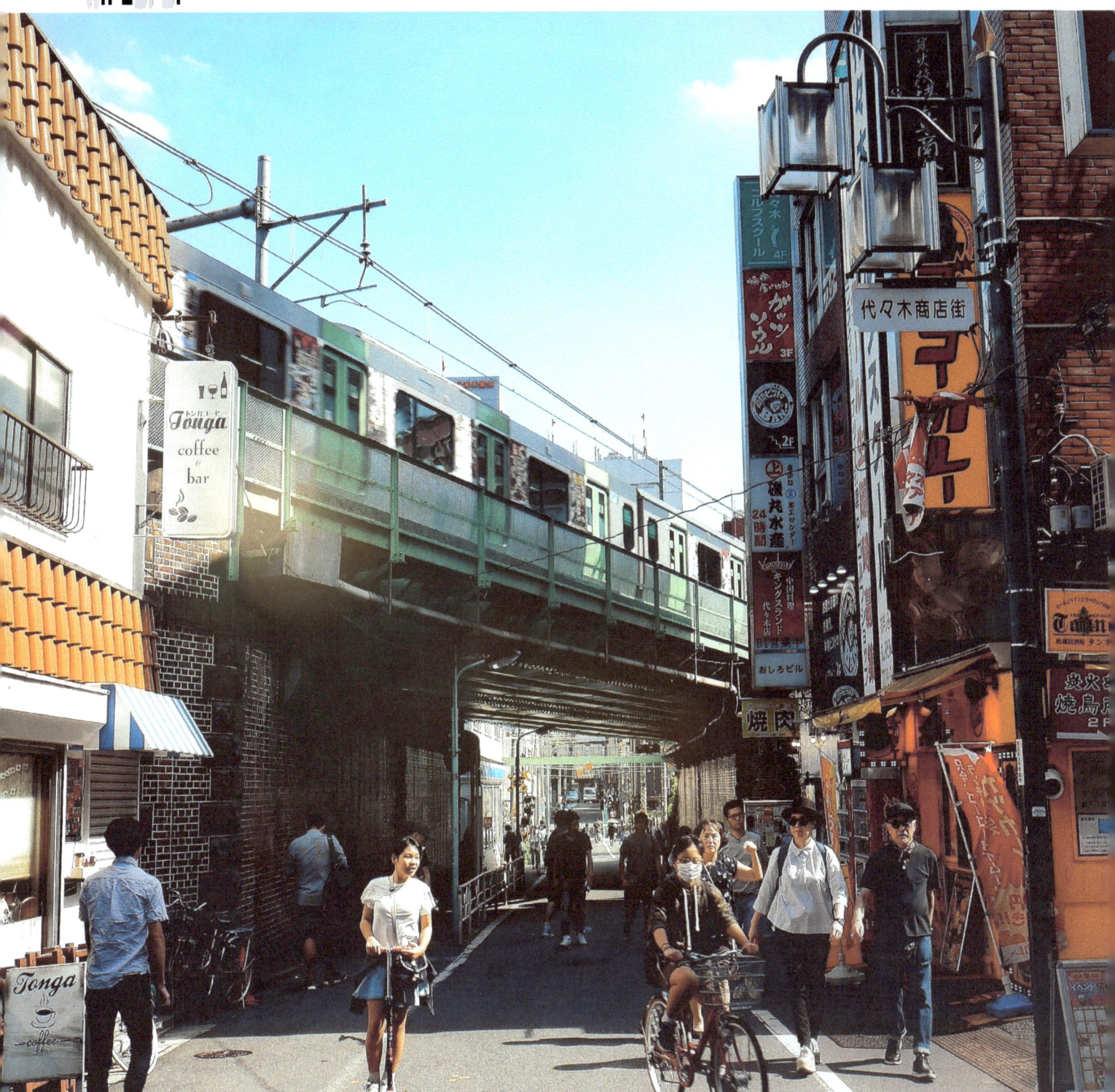
Photo by Mario Effendy

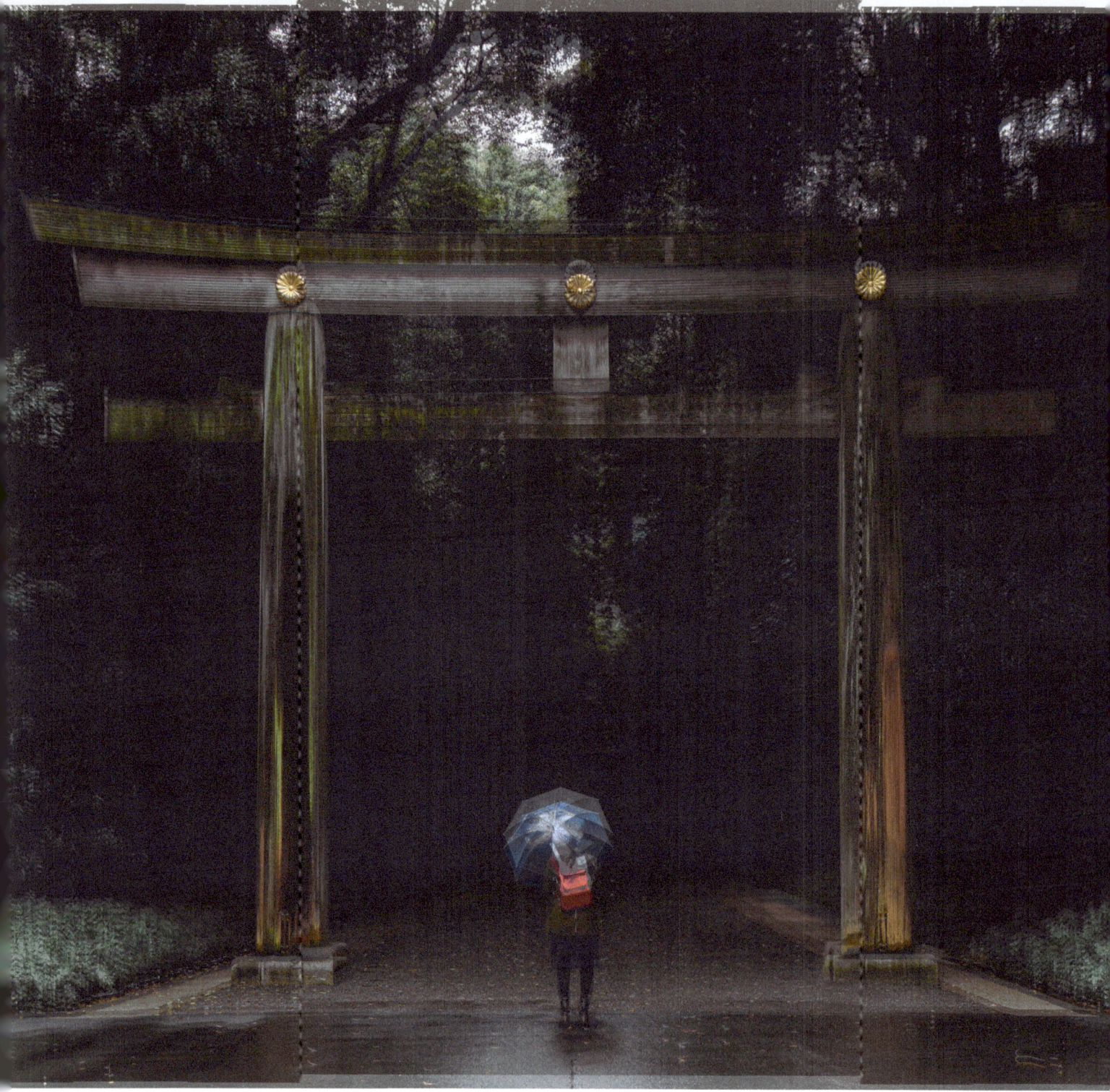

Photo by Michal Pechardo

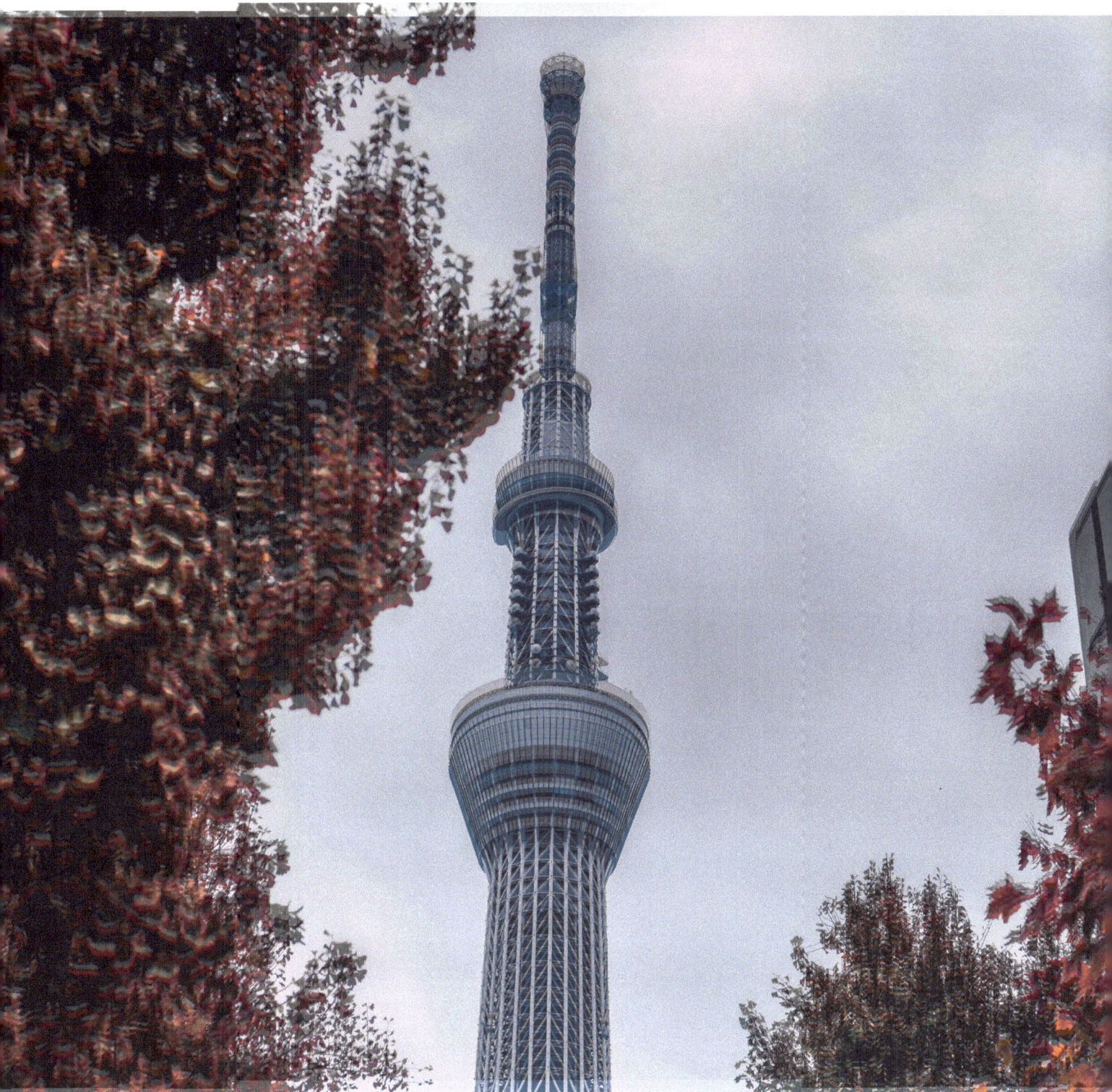
Photo by Charles Postiaux

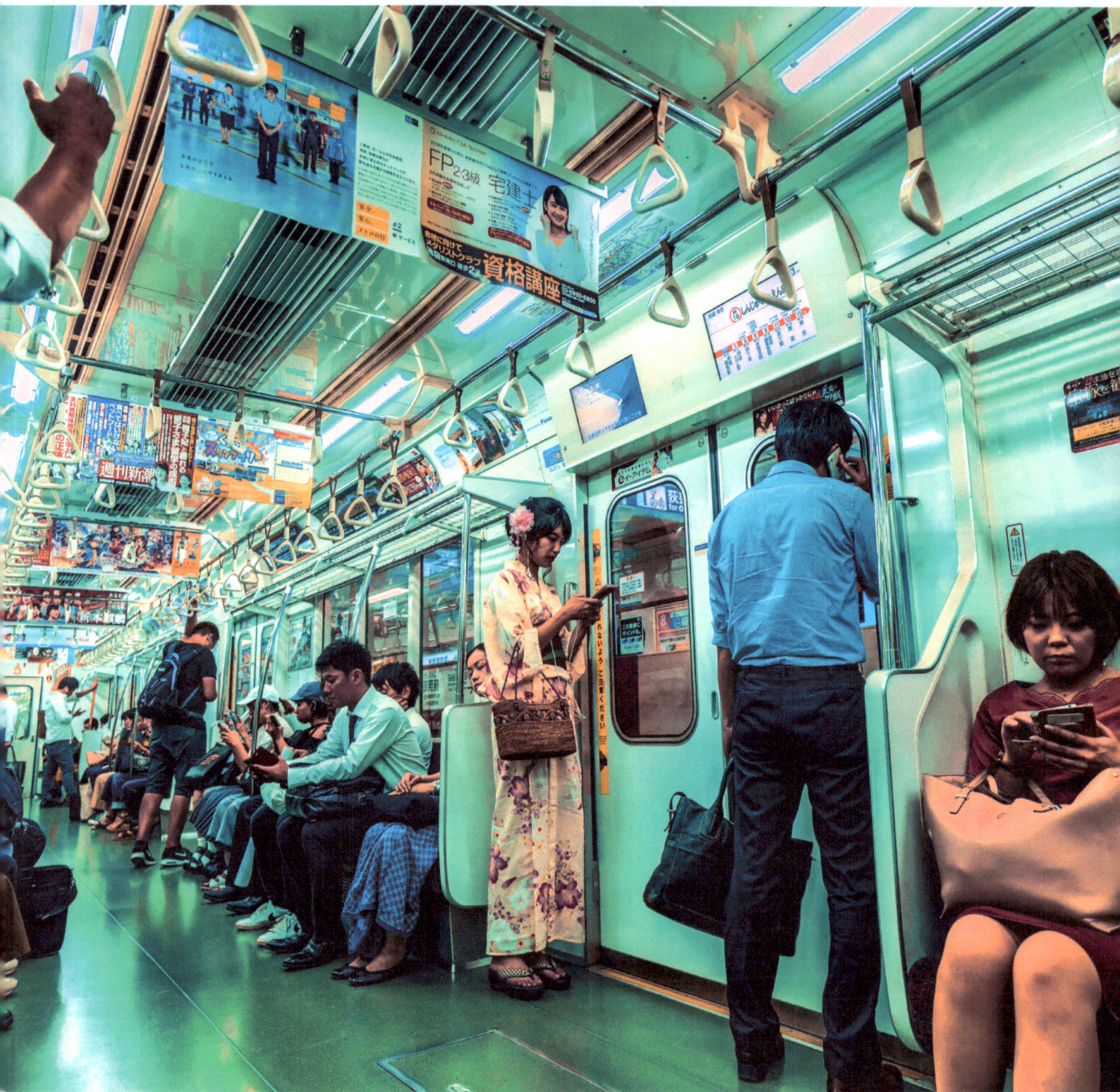
Photo by Jezael Melgoza

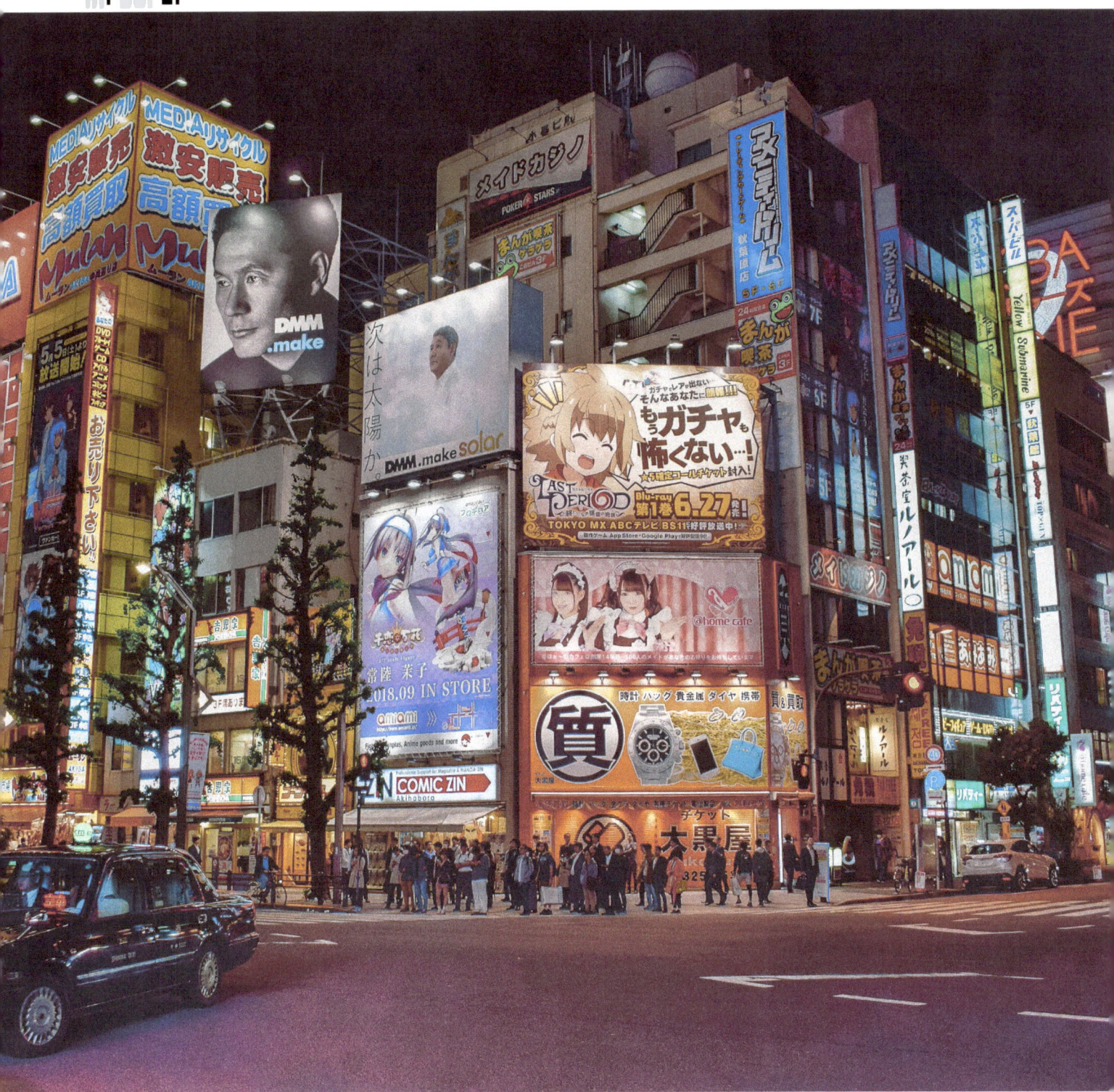

Photo by Dave Weatherall

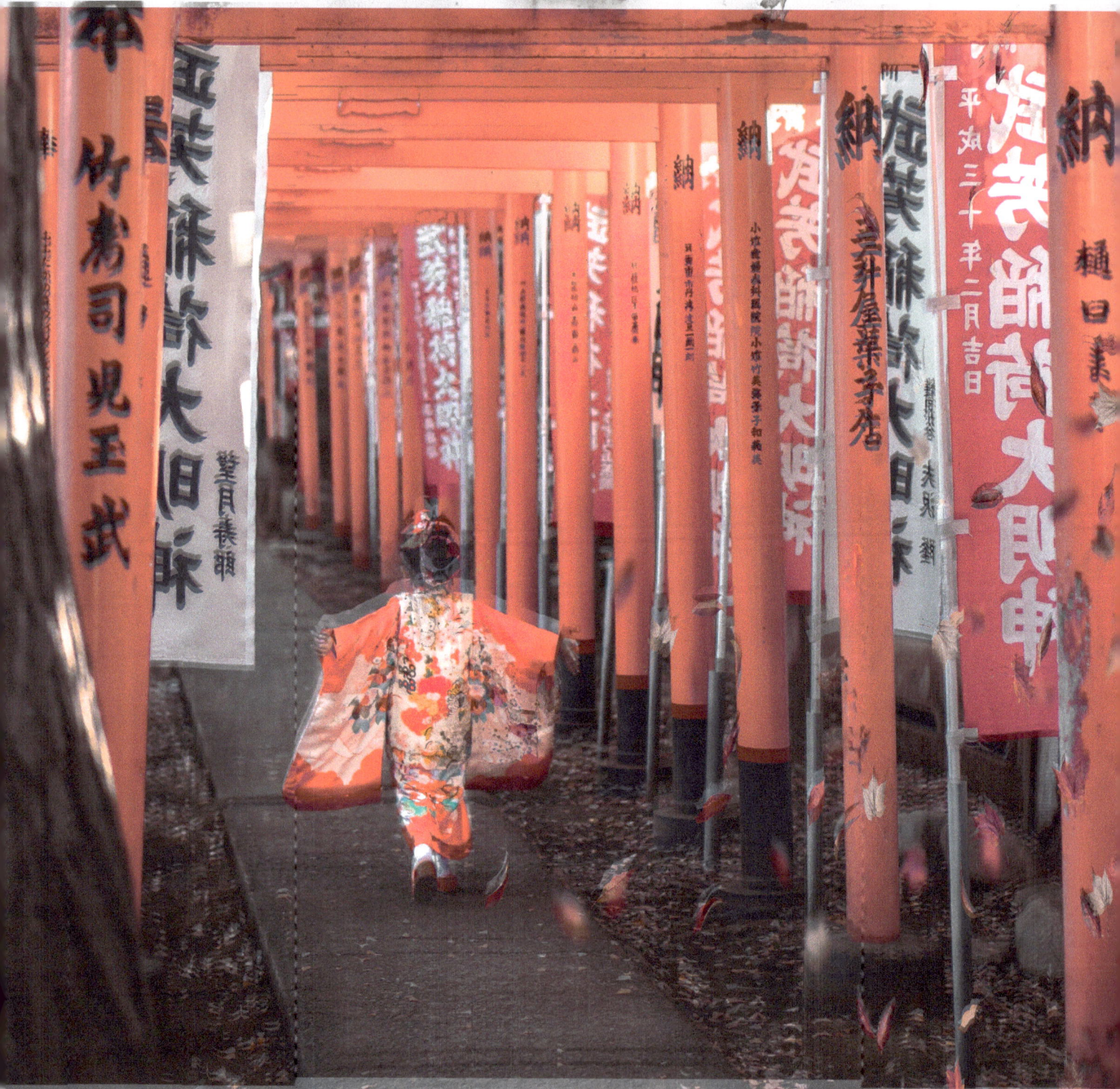
Photo by Eea Ikeda

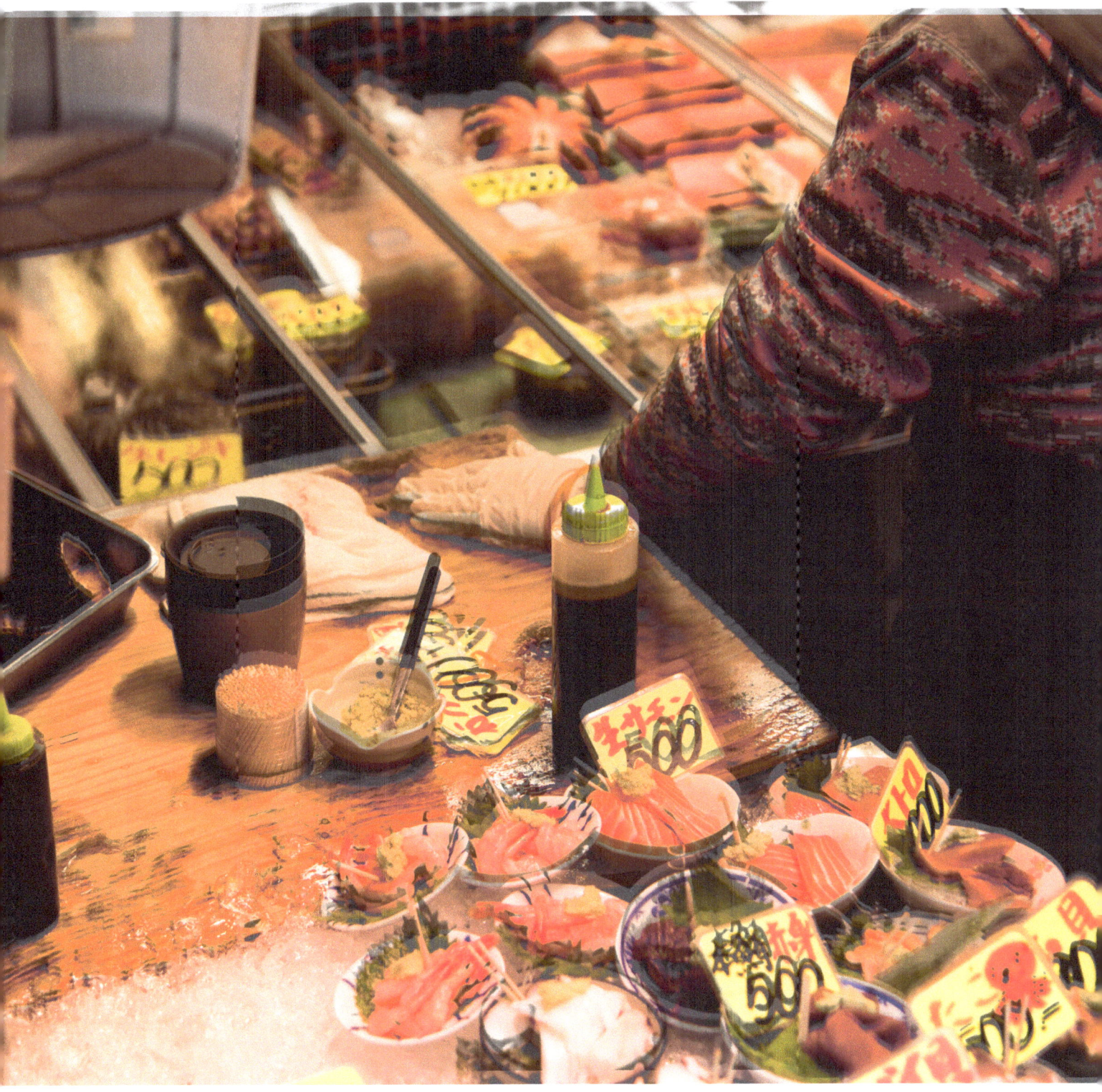

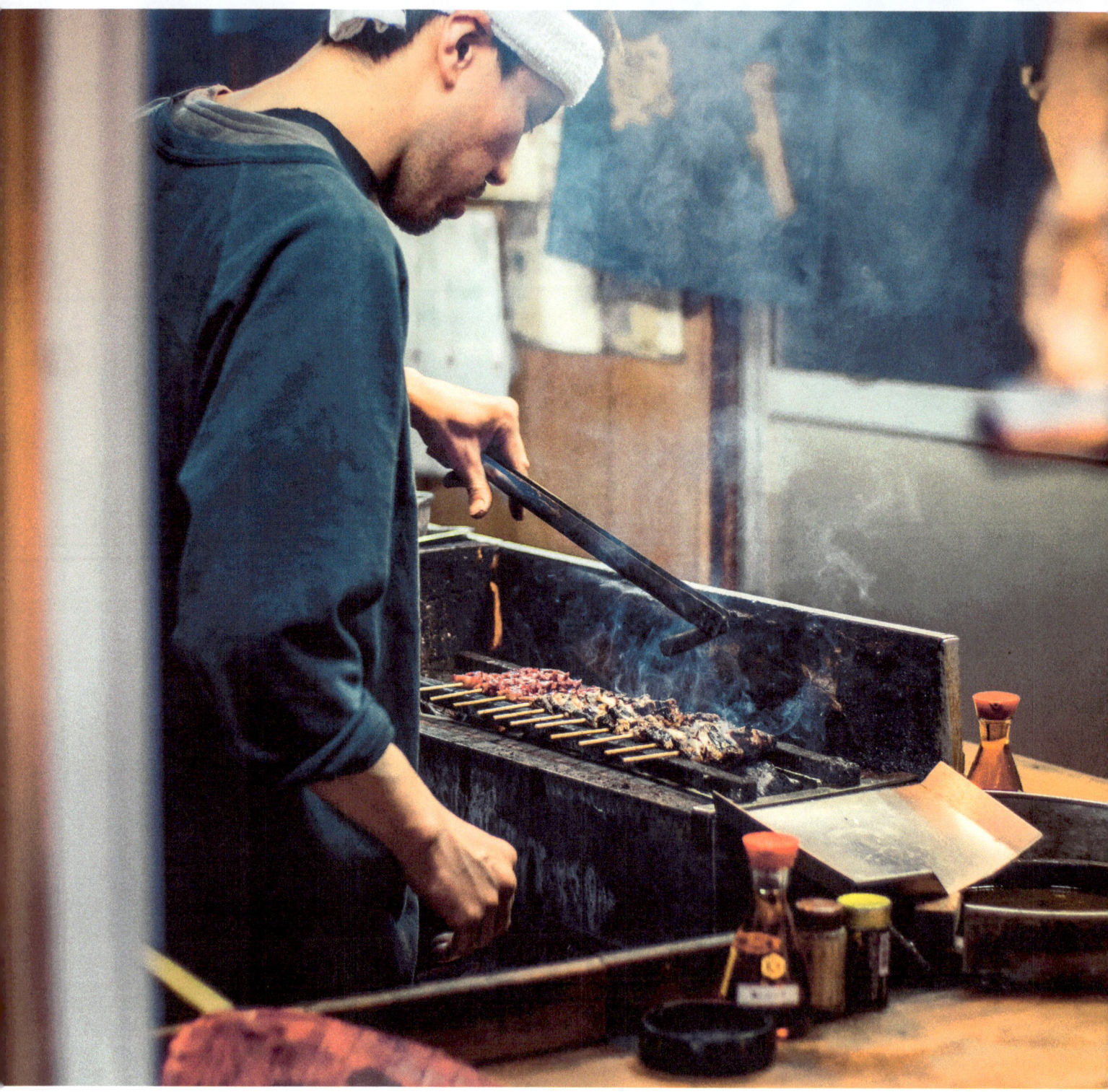
Photo by Gabriel Forsberg

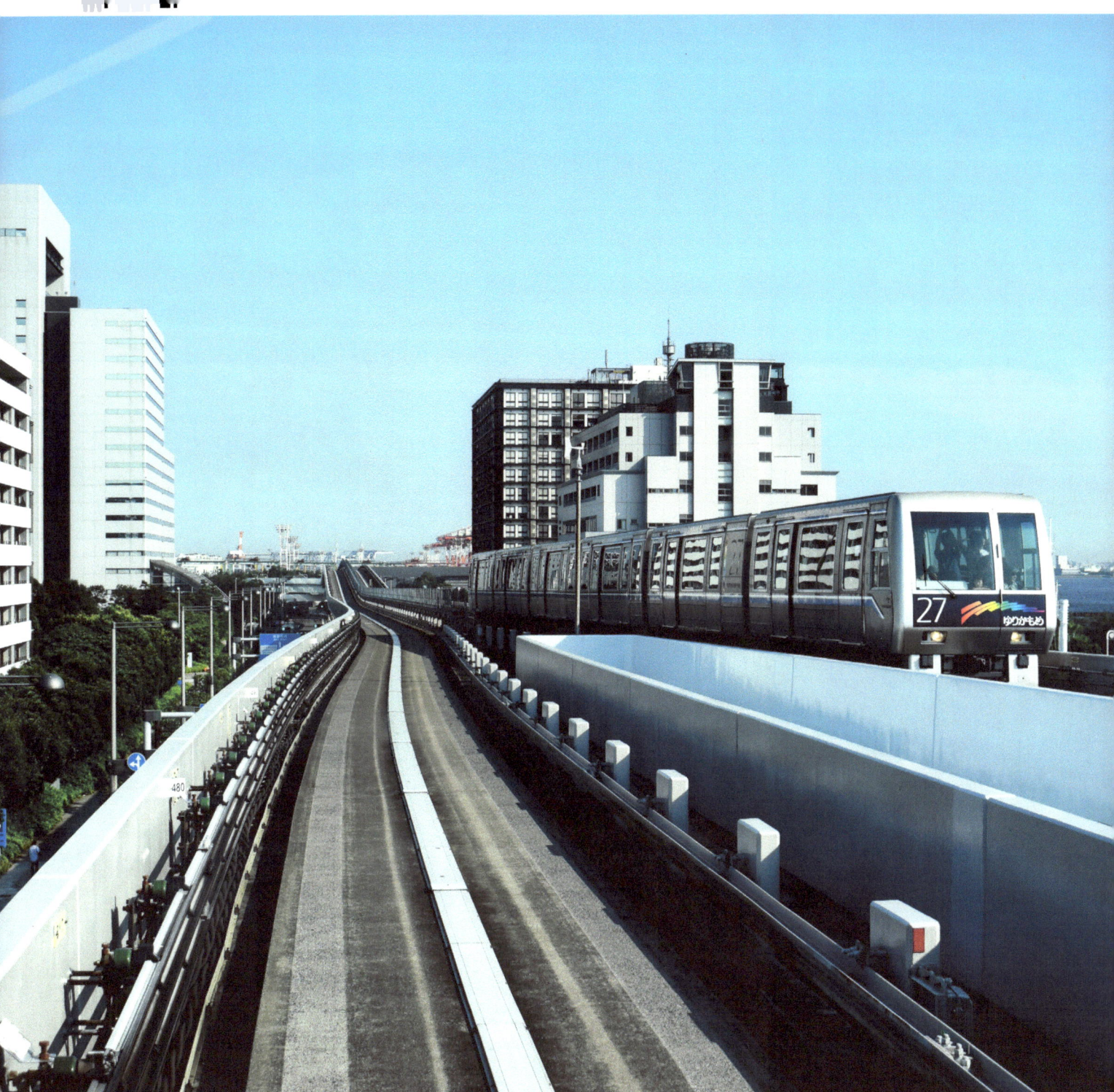
Photo by Chris Barbalis

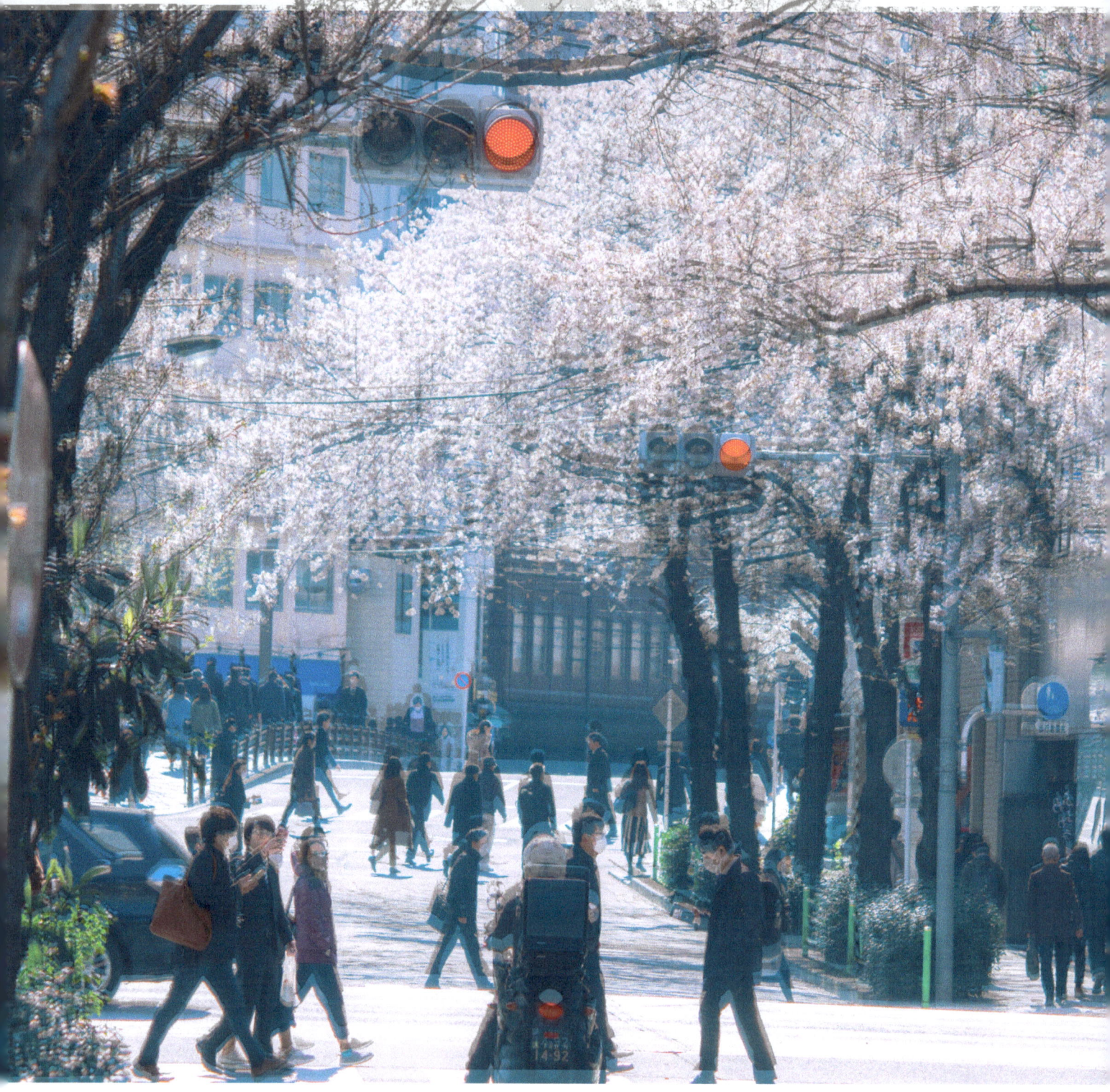
Photo by Atul Vinayak

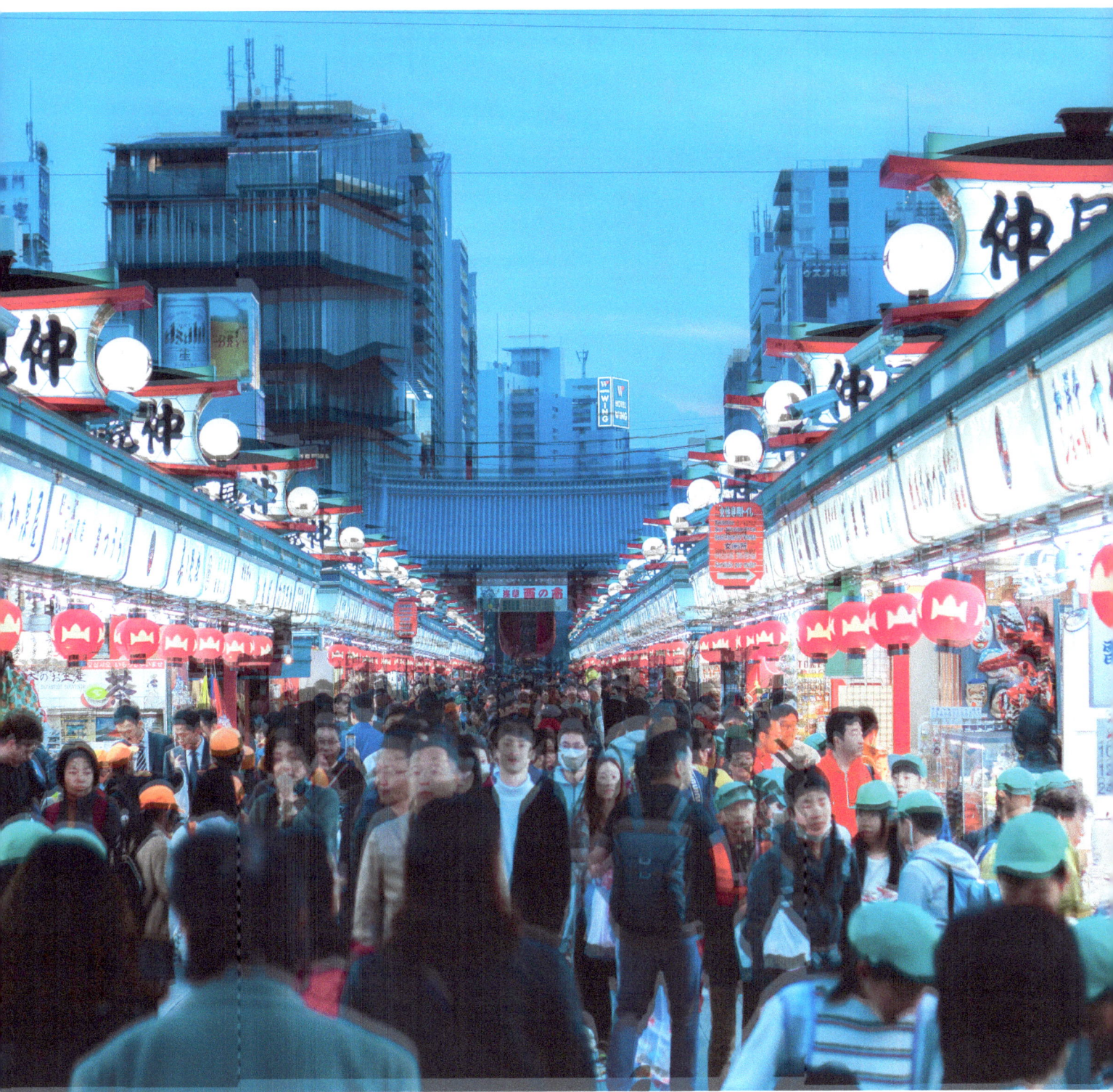
Photo by Benjamin Wong

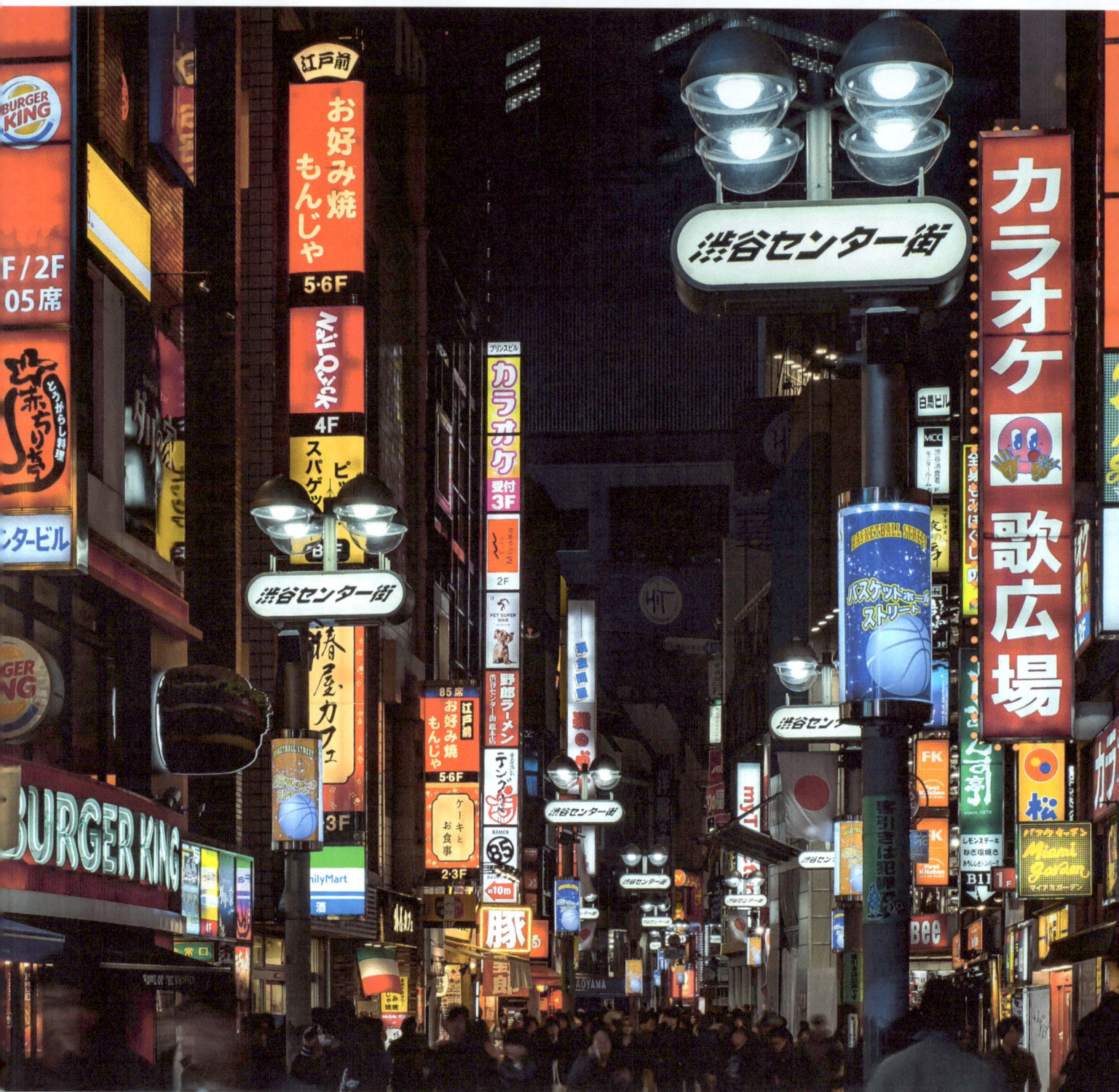

Photo by Pat Krupa

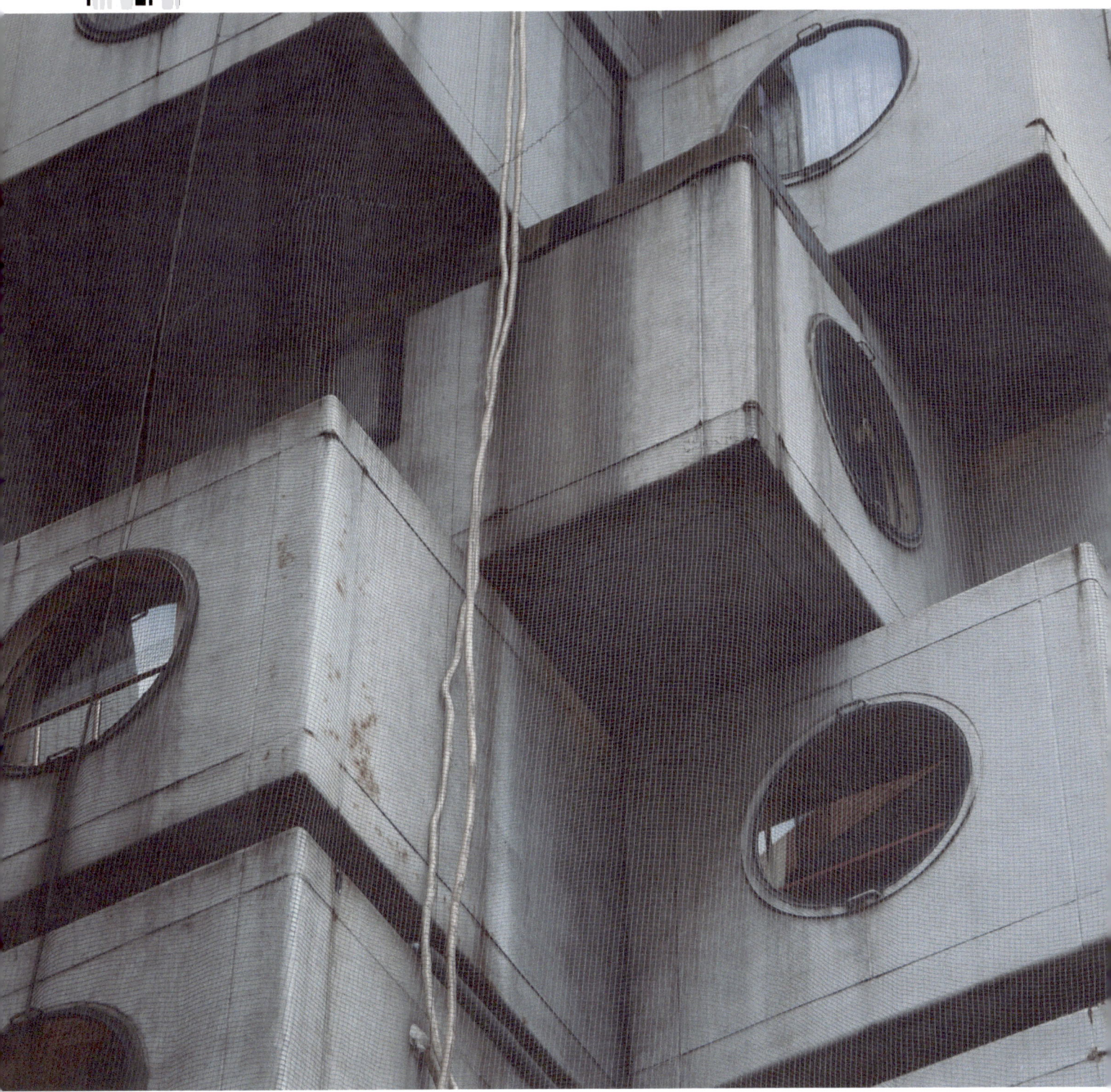
Photo by Michel Catalisano

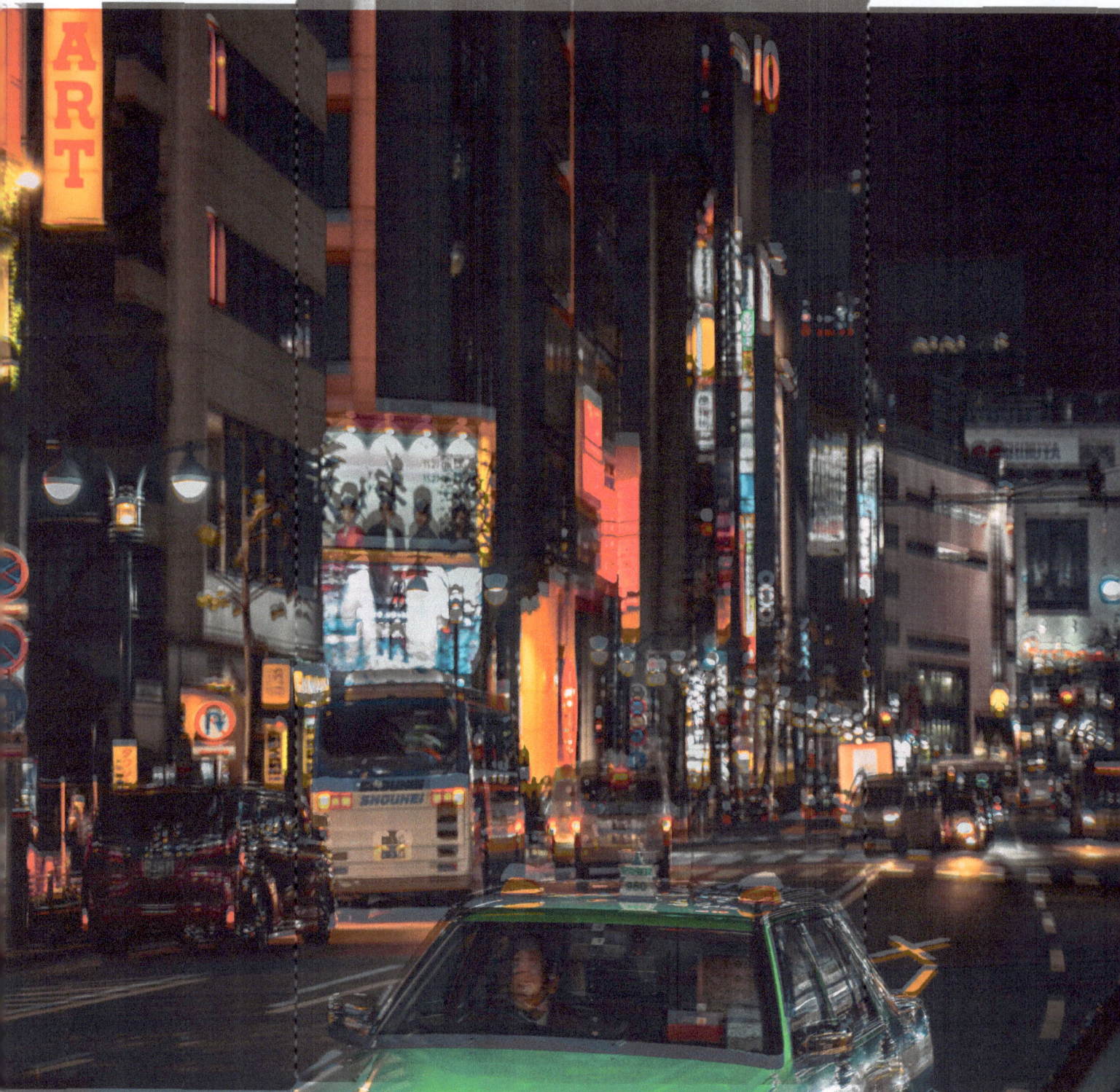
Photo by Heshan Perera

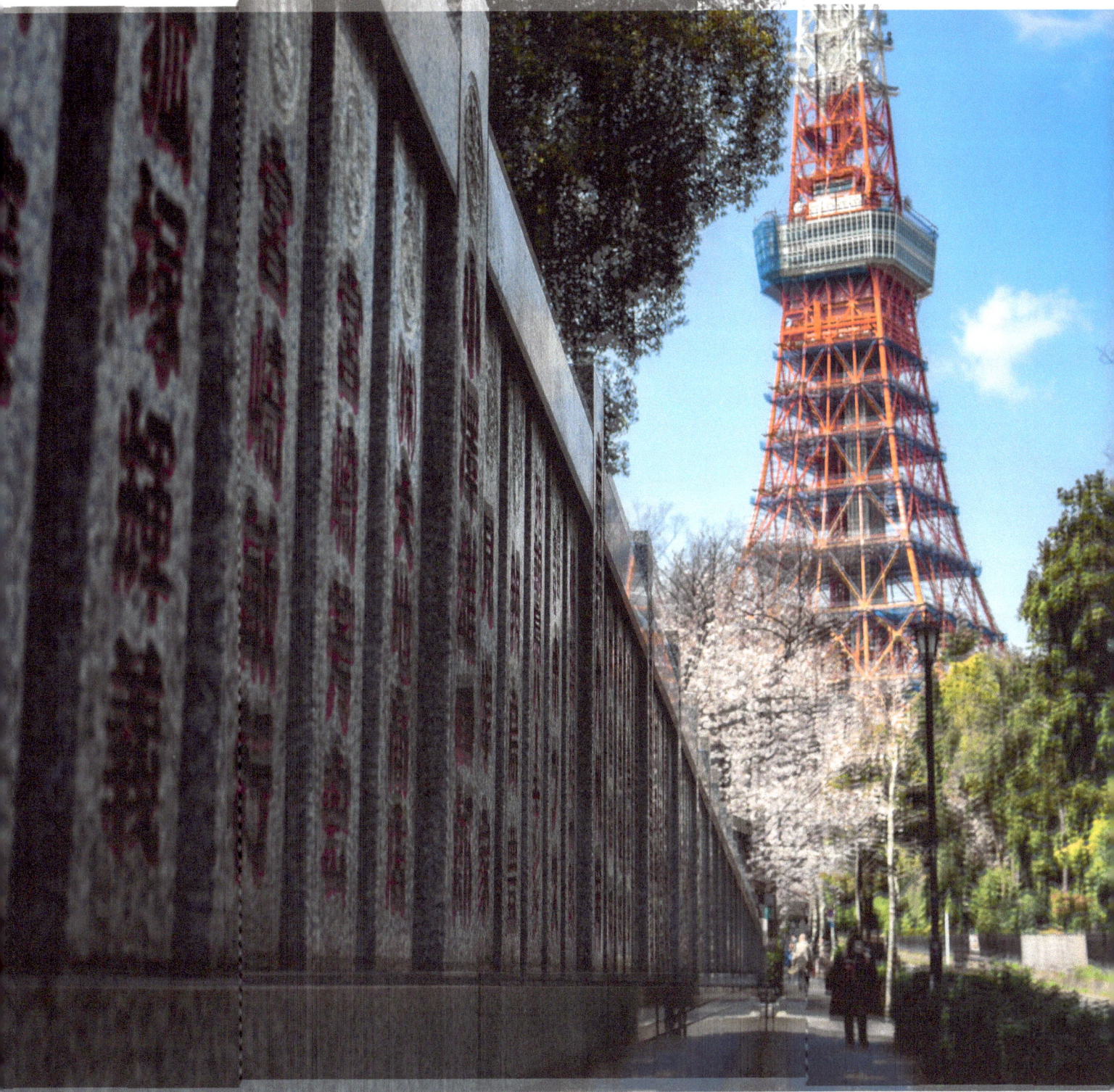

Photo by Yoav Aziz

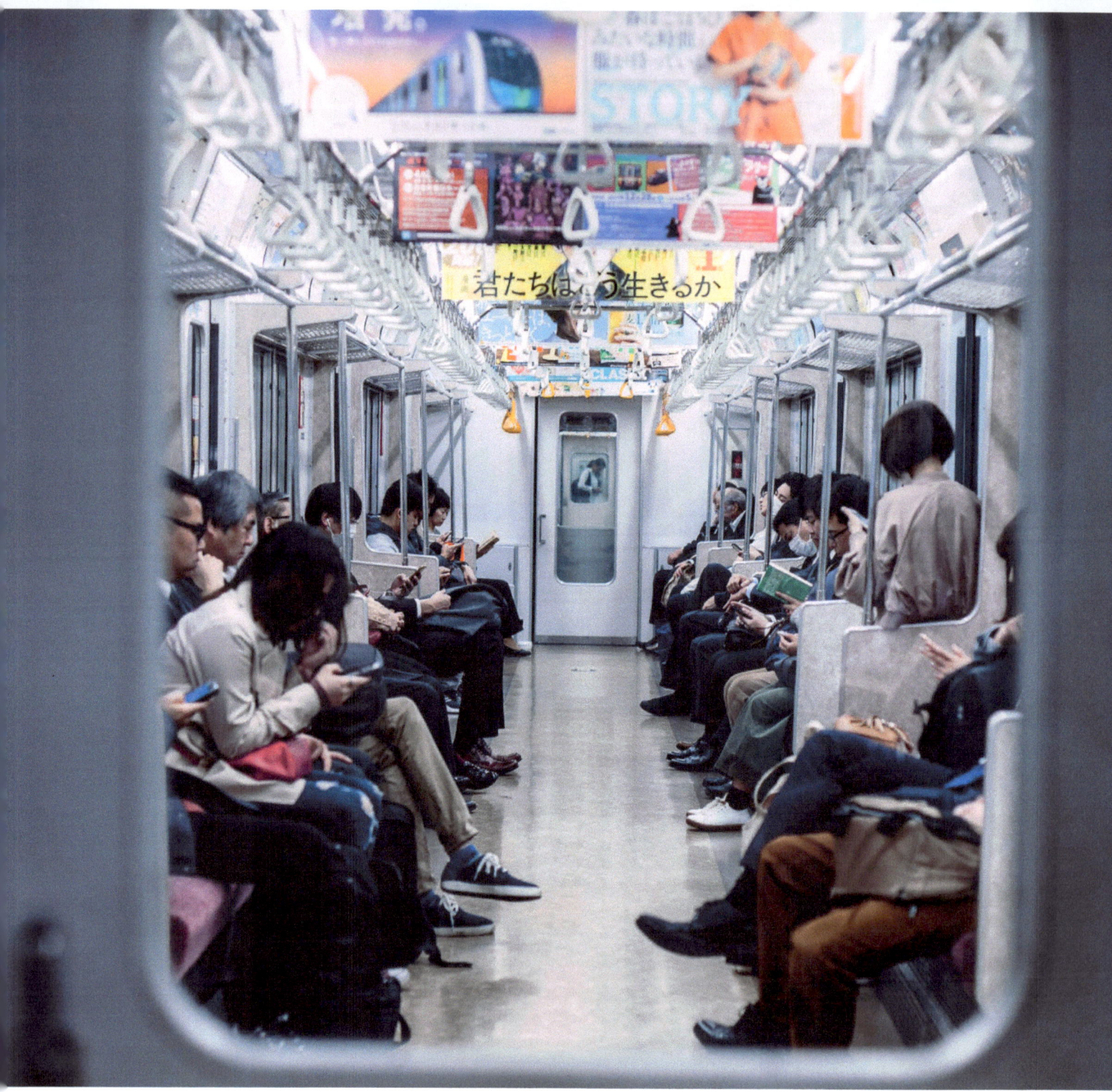

Photo by Liam Burnett Blue

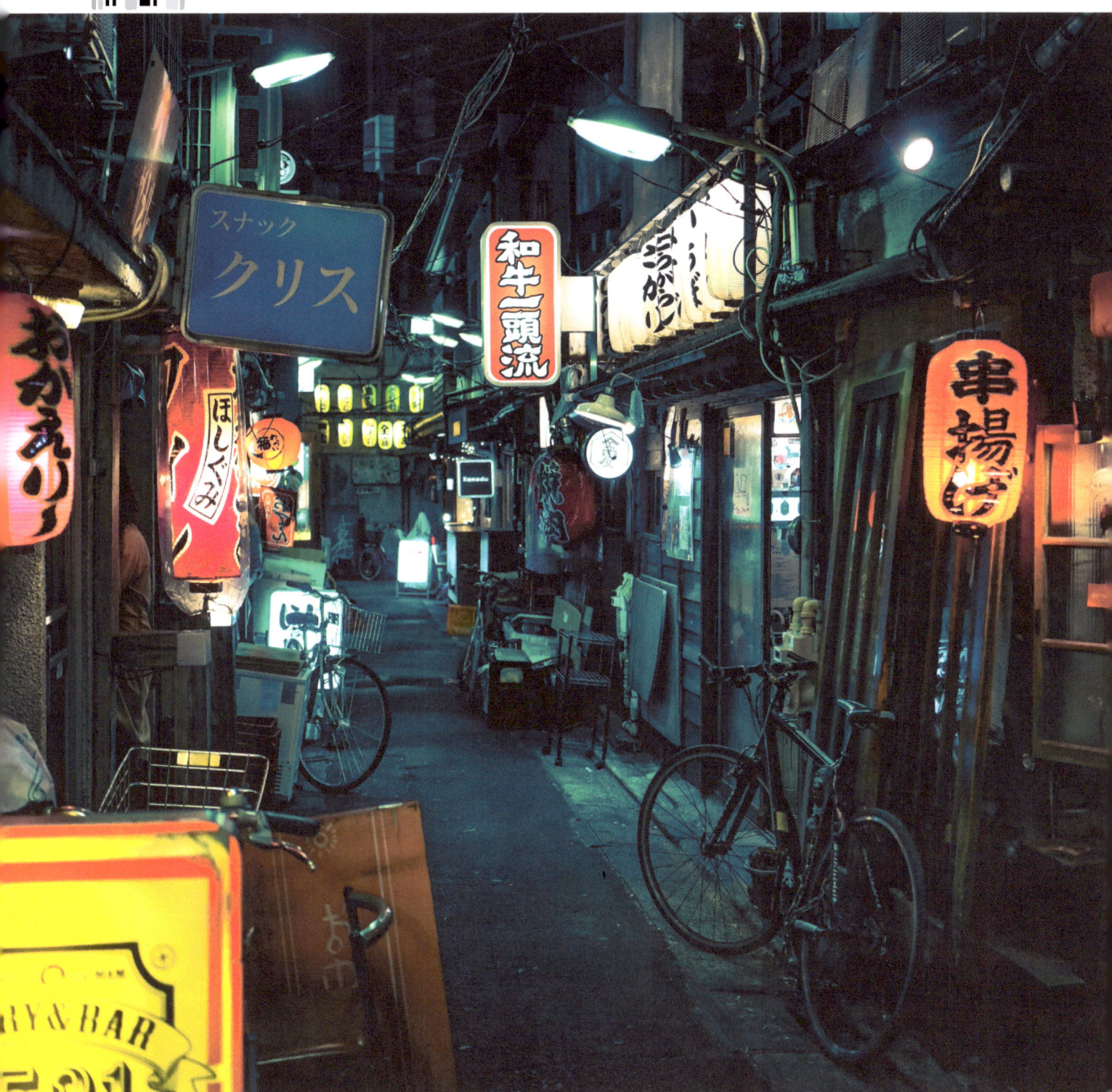

Photo by Alex Knight

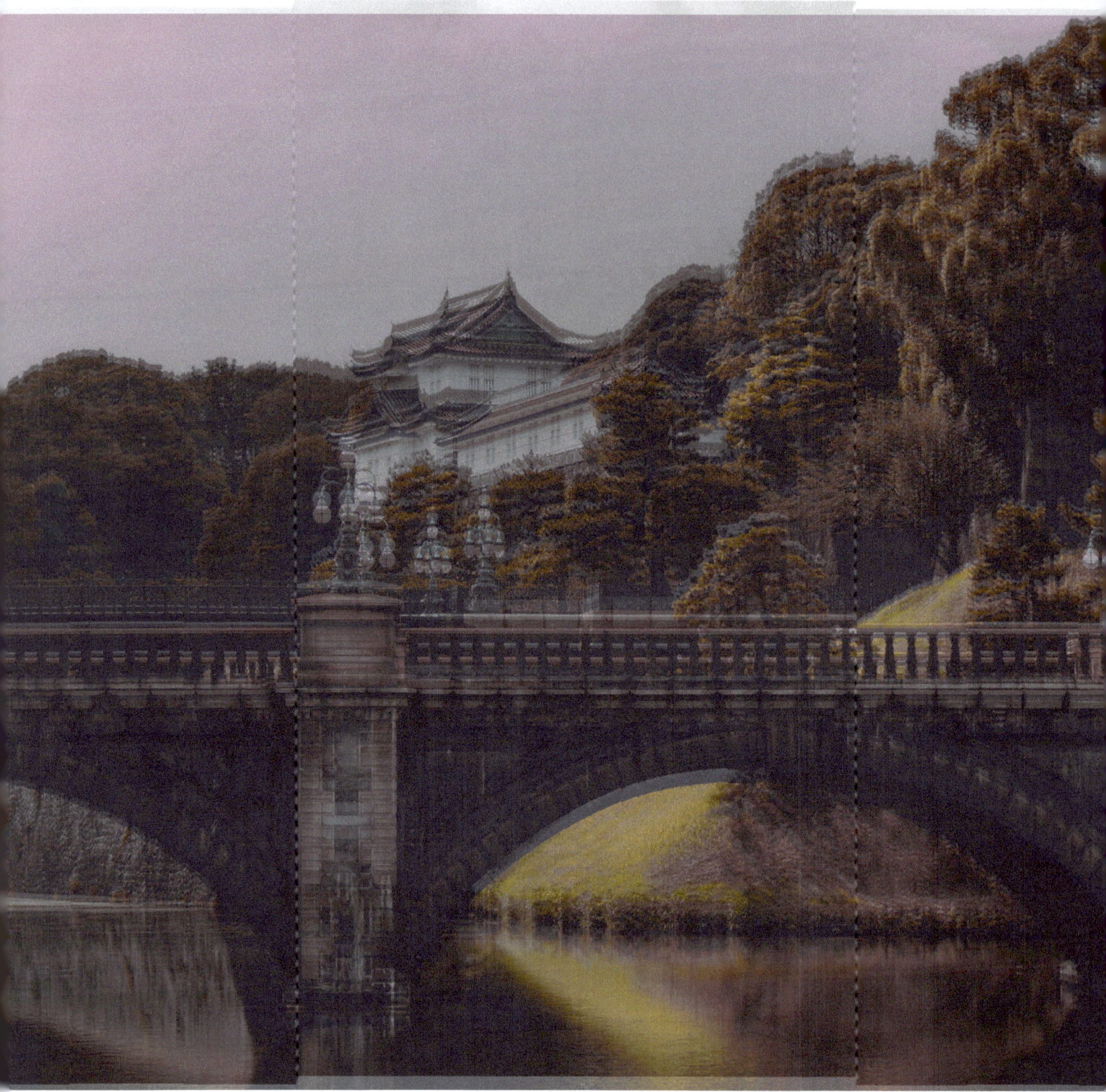
Photo by Alex P

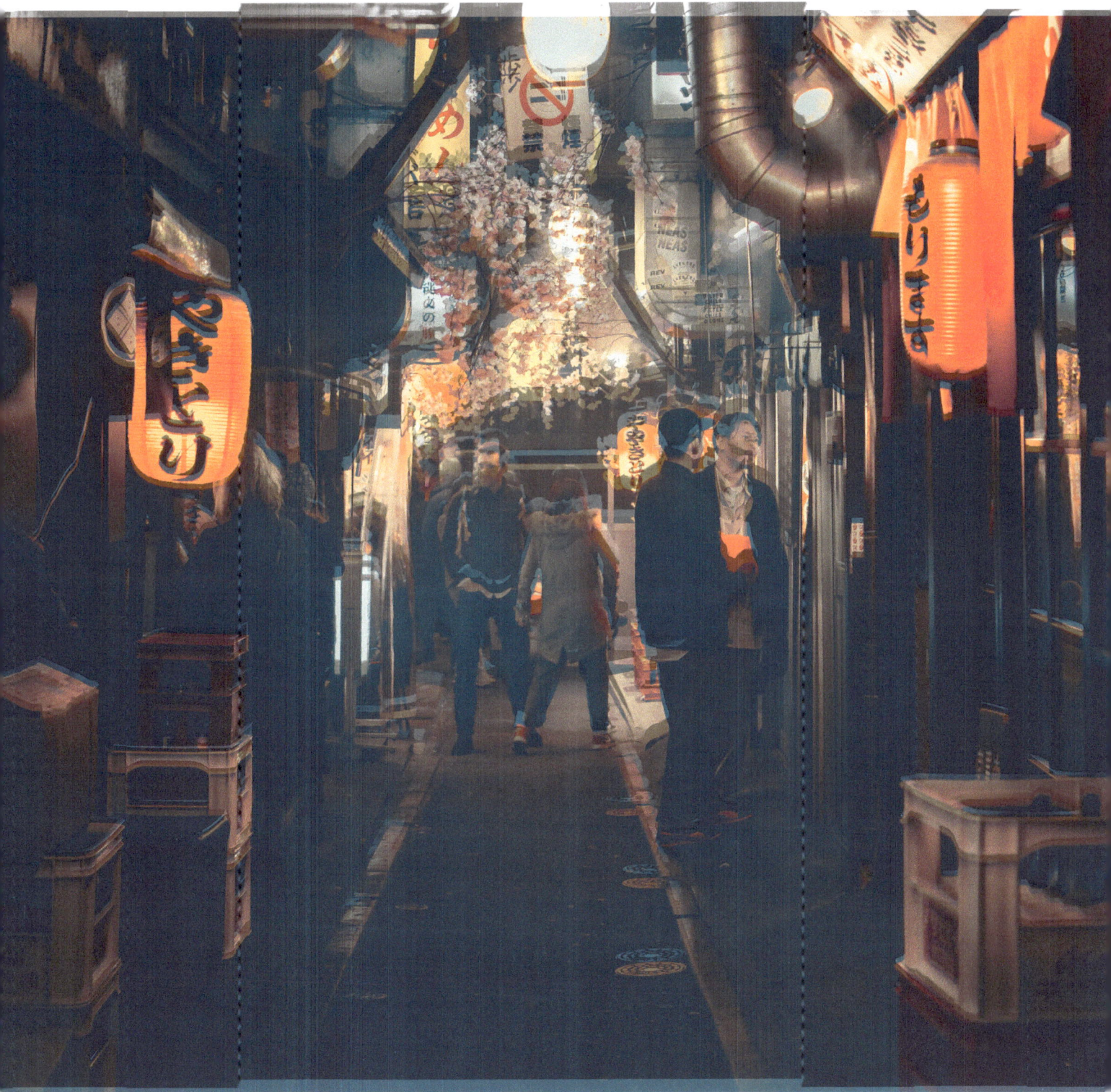
Photo By Yoav Aziz

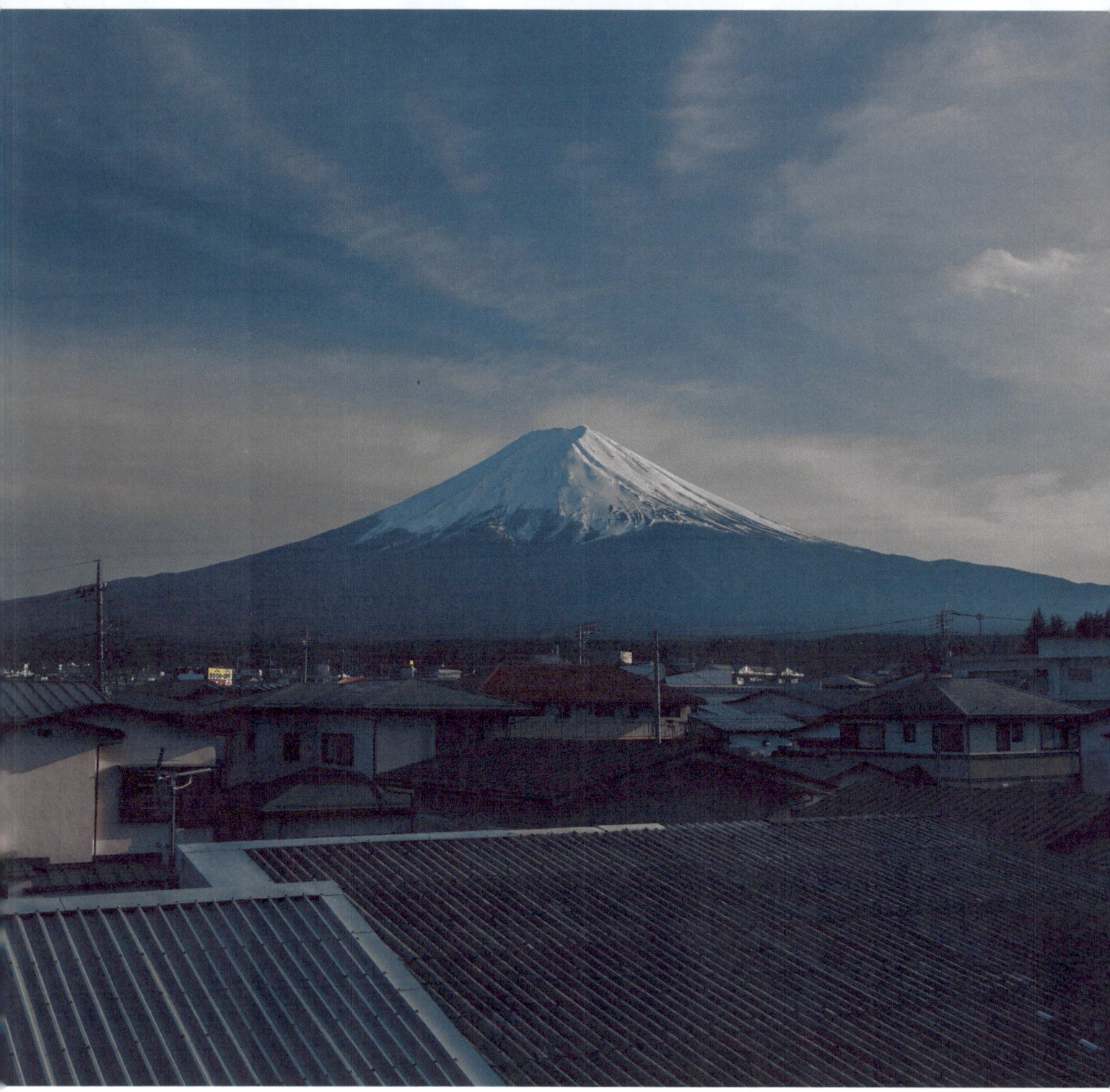
Photo by Chris Fowler

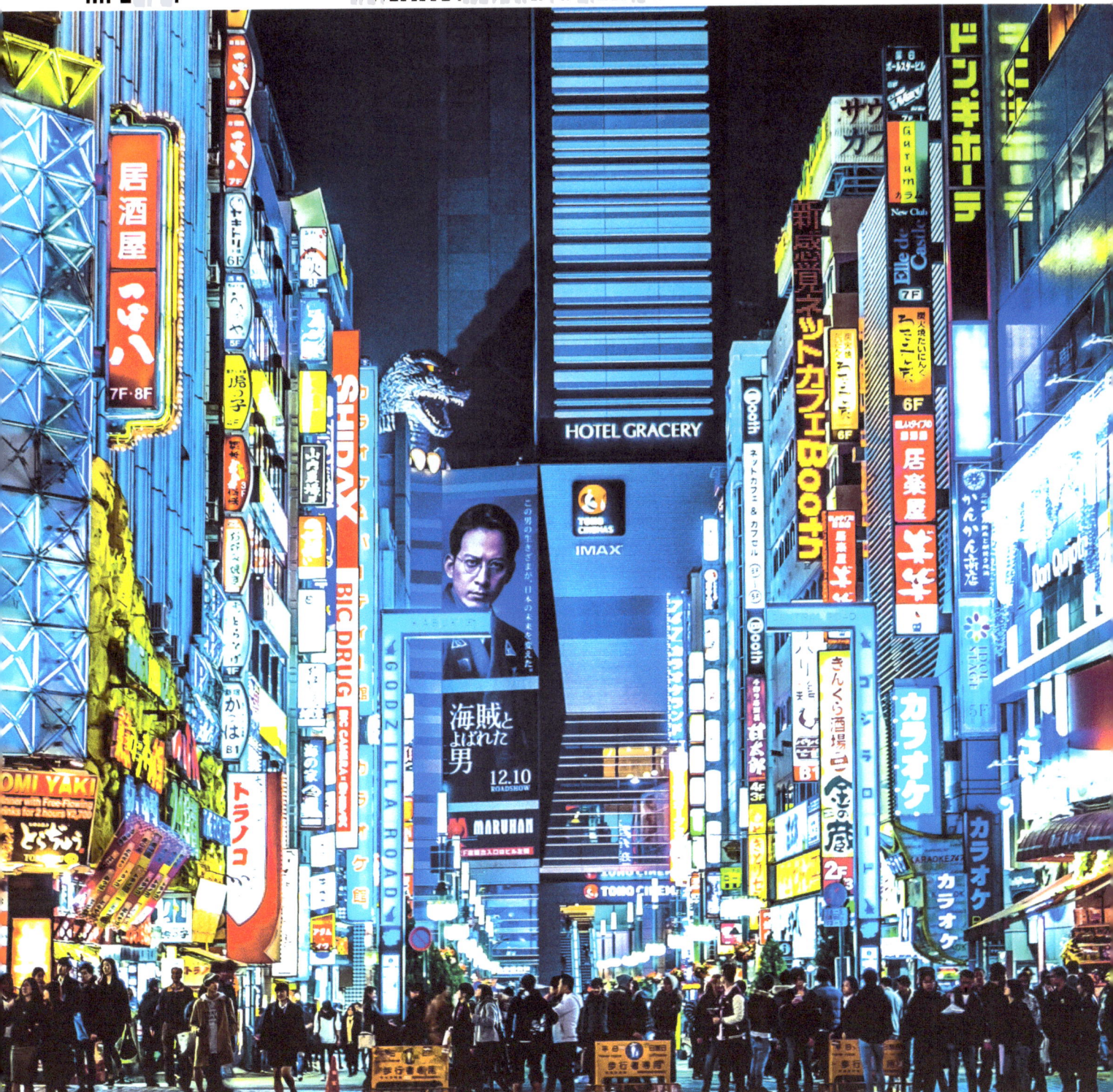
Photo by Erik Eastman

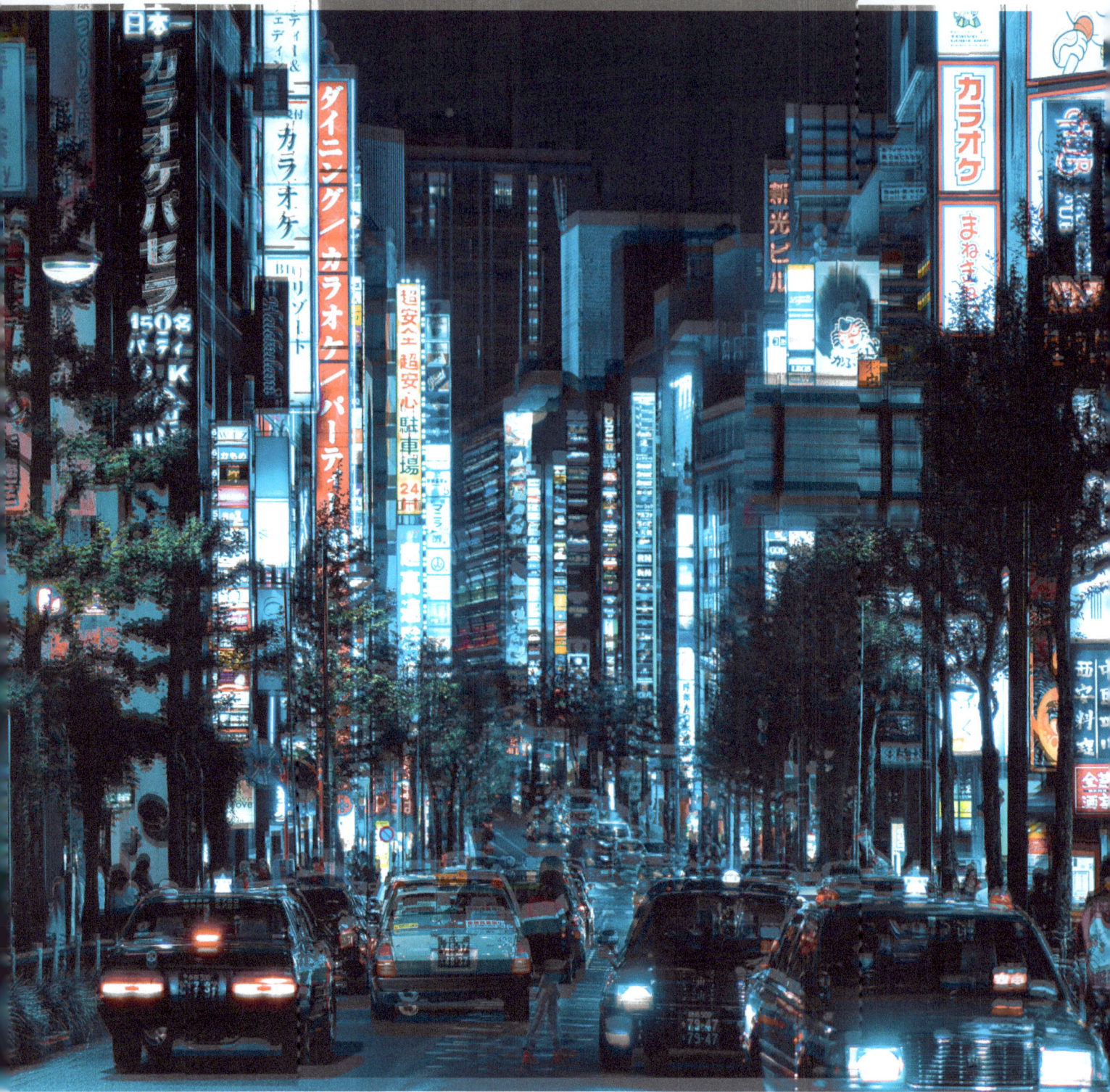
Photo by Berch

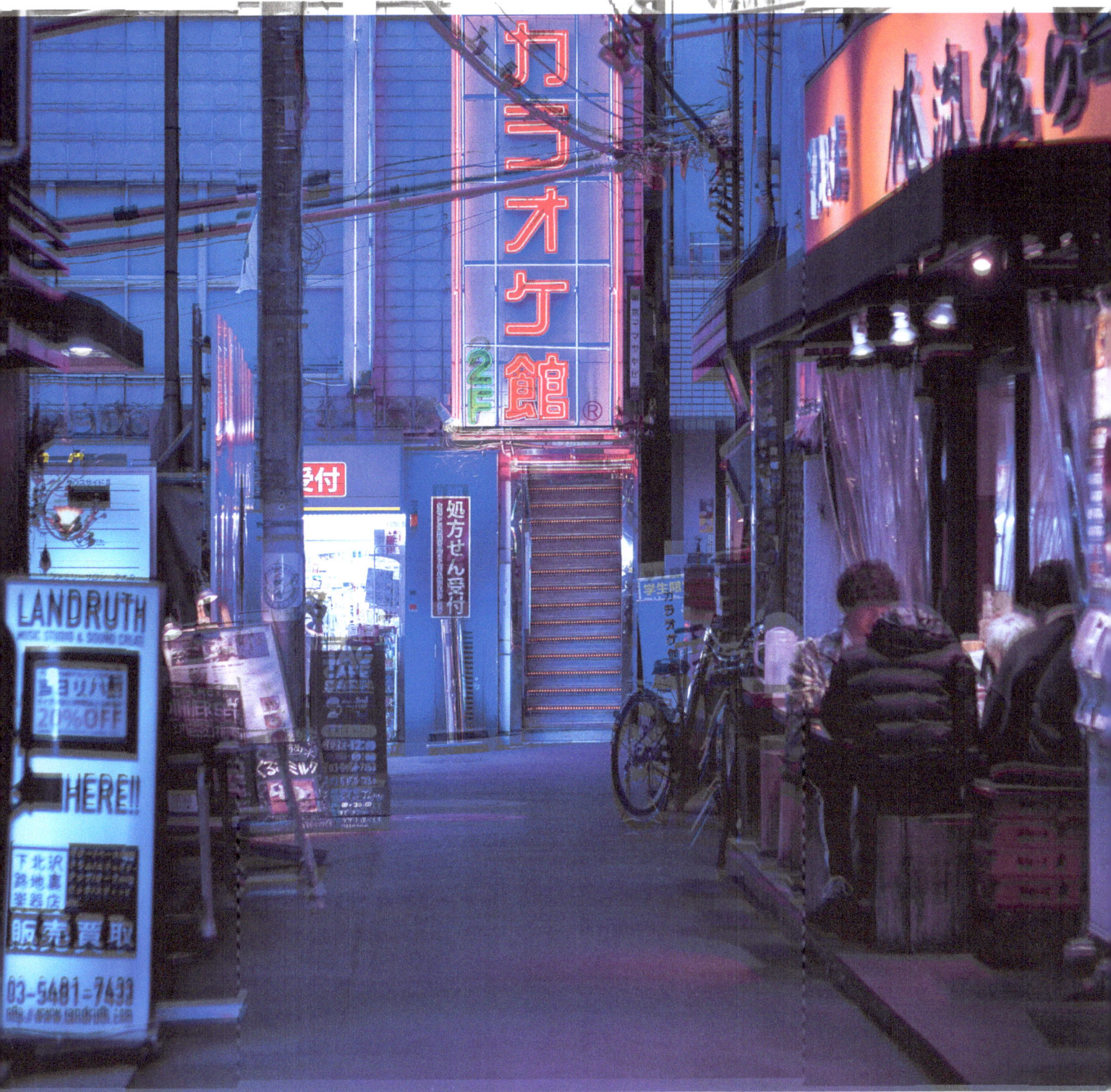

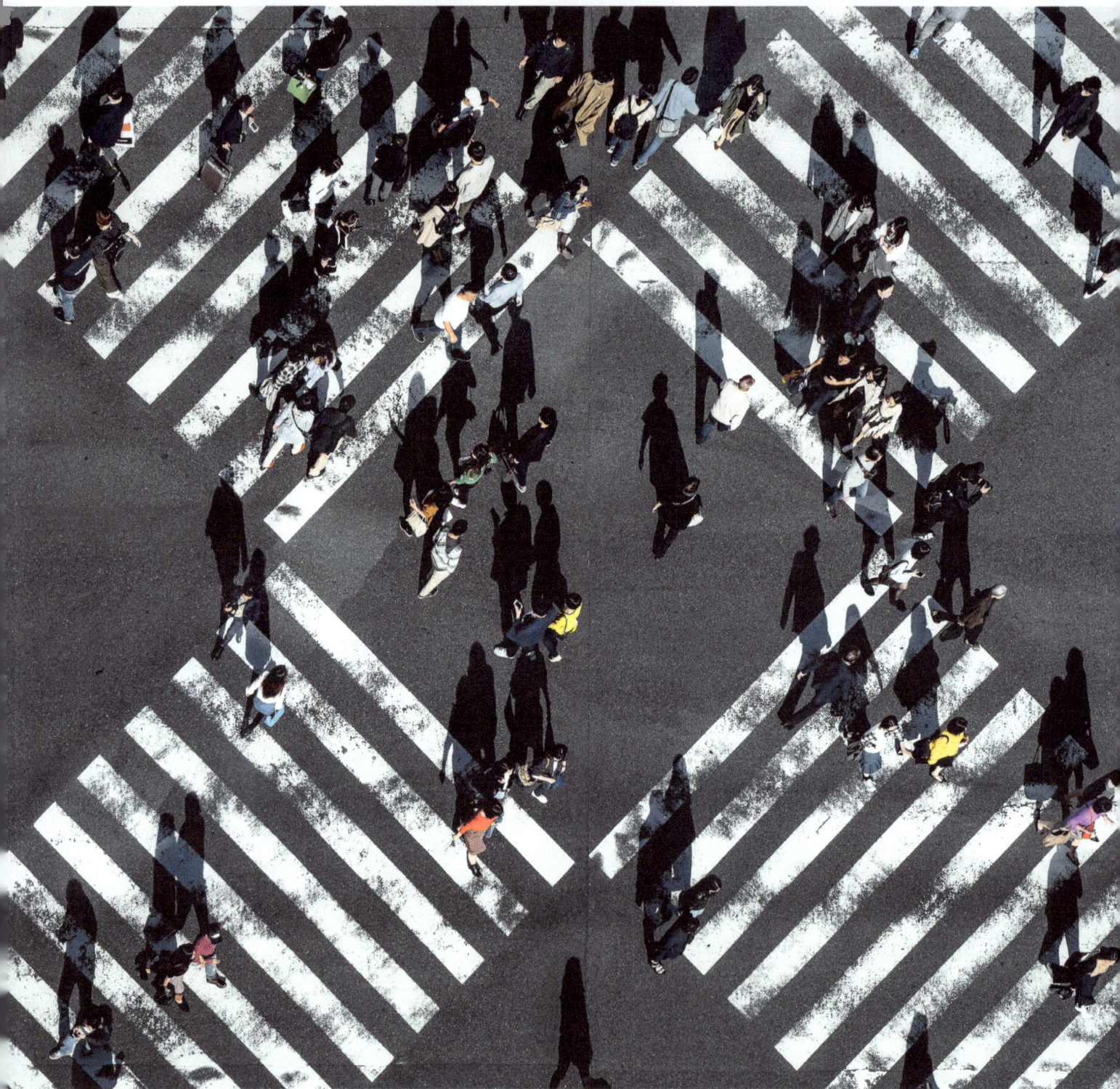
Photo by Ryoji Iwata

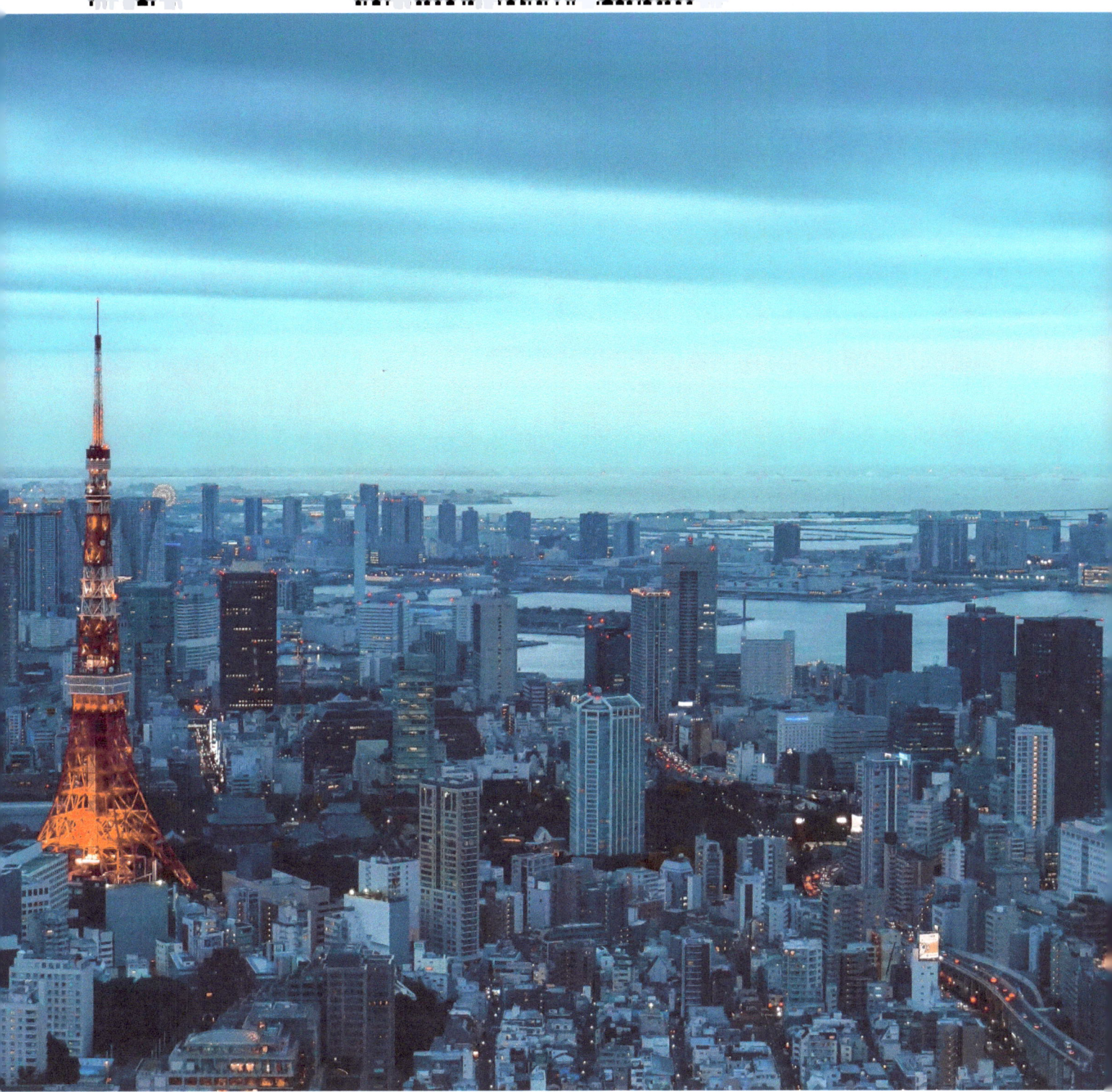
Photo by Louie Martinez

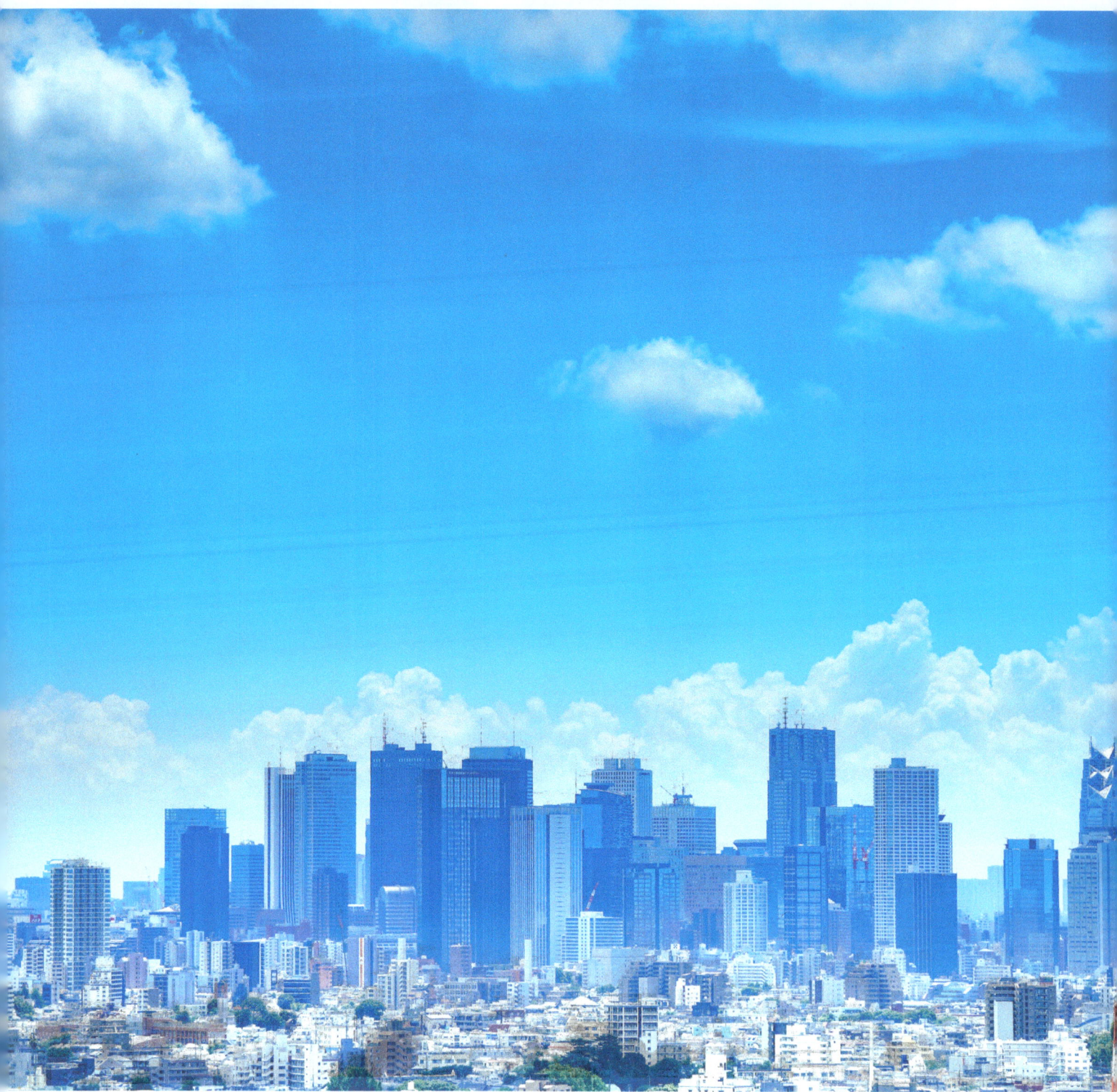
Photo by Ryo Yoshitake

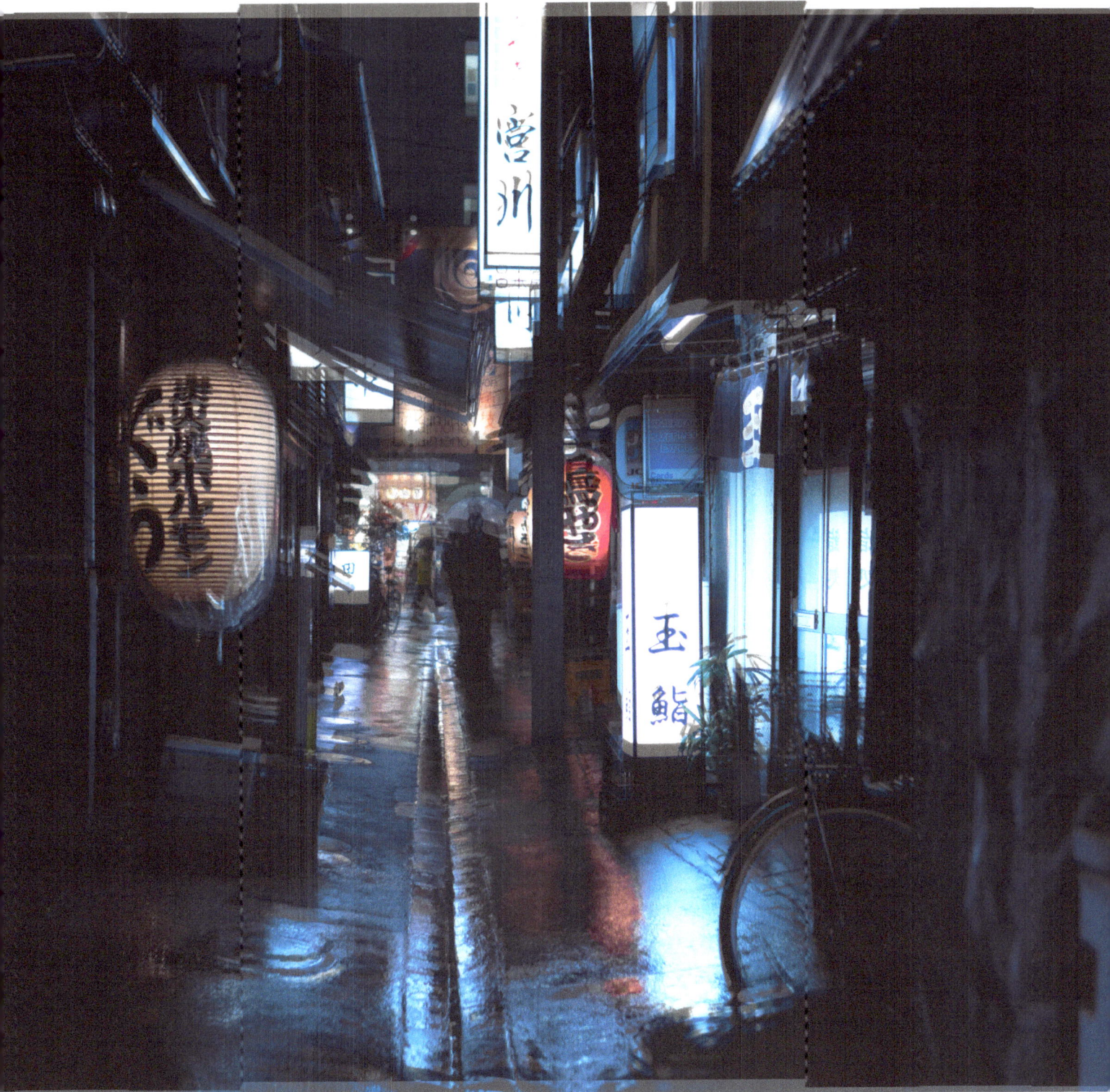
Photo by Simon Launay

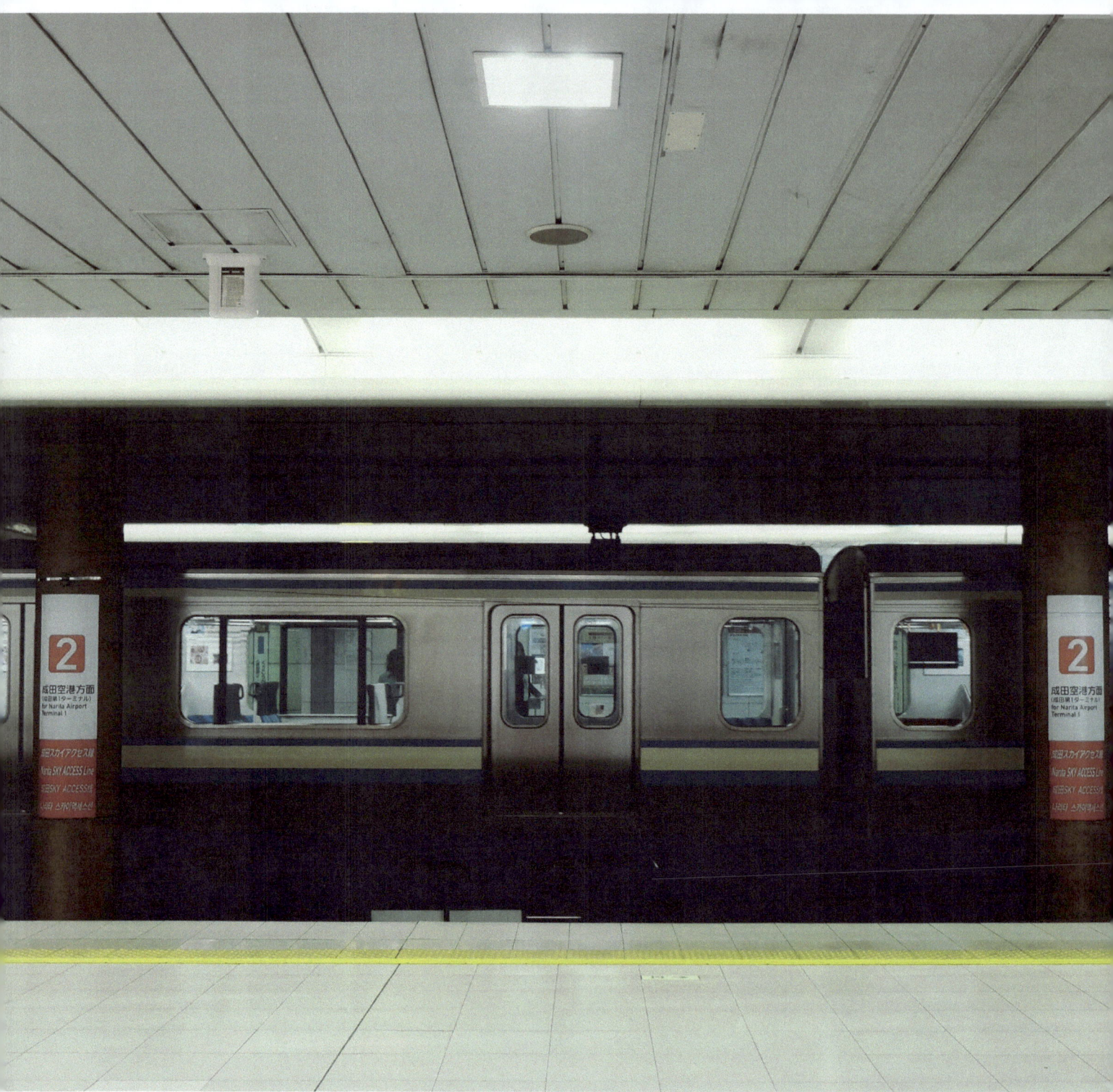
Photo by Lex Sirikiat

Other books in the City Porn Series:

Berlin
London
Los Angeles
New York
Paris

www.ingramcontent.com/pod-product-compliance
Lightning Source LLC
Chambersburg PA
CBHW051924210526
45473CB00006B/2123